NEGOTIATING

**FROM PLANNING YOUR STRATEGY
TO FINDING A COMMON GROUND,**
AN ESSENTIAL GUIDE TO
THE **ART OF NEGOTIATING**

101

NEGOTIATING 101

FROM **PLANNING YOUR STRATEGY** TO **FINDING A COMMON GROUND,** AN ESSENTIAL GUIDE TO THE **ART OF NEGOTIATING**

101

PETER SANDER, MBA

ADAMS MEDIA

NEW YORK   LONDON   TORONTO   SYDNEY   NEW DELHI

Adams Media
An Imprint of Simon & Schuster, Inc.
100 Technology Center Drive
Stoughton, MA 02072

First Adams Media hardcover edition JUNE 2017

ADAMS MEDIA and colophon are trademarks of Simon and Schuster.

For information about special discounts for bulk purchases, please contact Simon &
Schuster Special Sales at 1-866-506-1949 or business@simonandschuster.com.

The Simon & Schuster Speakers Bureau can bring authors to your live event. For more
information or to book an event contact the Simon & Schuster Speakers Bureau at
1-866-248-3049 or visit our website at www.simonspeakers.com.

Manufactured in the United States of America

7 2022

Library of Congress Cataloging-in-Publication Data has been applied for.

ISBN 978-1-5072-0269-2
ISBN 978-1-5072-0270-8 (ebook)

Dedication

Negotiating professionals, which includes most of you, far outnumber professional negotiators. It is mainly to you that I dedicate this book.

Contents

INTRODUCTION

Like most people, you work for a living. You run a small business. Or you're a position player in a larger one. Or you're employed in a nonprofit or public agency. Or perhaps you're not part of the work force at all.

Sooner or later (most likely sooner) you will need or want *something* from someone else. That someone else might be another individual, another organization, or an individual or organization inside or outside your business or organization. As for what you need or what, it could be a new hire, a labor deal, a supply of raw material, a professional consultation, financial advice, or even a meeting room. You need something from someone, and it's important.

That something may be large or it may be small. Now you have to meet with someone to obtain it. Since resources are precious, you have to try to get the best deal. You'll have to do a little "give and take" to get the best value for your money, the best value for your time, the best value for whatever resources you have to offer.

You have to *negotiate*.

It *sounds* scary. We hear of tense, drawn-out negotiations about labor agreements or peace talks to stop wars. The very idea of being on stage with such high stakes in the balance would scare most of us to death.

Fortunately most of our negotiations in real life are smaller and less critical—but still important. A meeting or two, even a phone call or exchange of emails might do it. In today's ever-faster business world, rapid-fire technology tools accelerate the speed of negotiations.

But however brief the negotiations, and no matter what you're negotiating for, you still need to know what you're doing. You want a deal that meets your needs, one that creates the value you seek without giving away the store.

That's where *Negotiating 101* comes in. This book gives you the basic tools, skills, defenses, and processes to become a more confident and effective negotiator—whether it's your full-time job or something you do once in a while, and whether it's for a $10 million contract at work or the use of the family car with your teenage boys.

The same principles apply.

THE MAIN IDEA(S)

Negotiating 101 covers the main ideas, strategies, tactics, responses, and skills to help you through any kind of negotiation with any counterparty, anywhere. The underlying principles and themes of negotiation you'll see throughout the book include:

- *Negotiating is everywhere.* You negotiate while at work, at home, even during leisure activities. You may negotiate contracts for jetliners, for cleaning services, or with your kids for dinnertime; these are all negotiations. They differ in size and scope only, but not the basics.
- *Negotiating may be your profession, but more likely it is part of your profession.* A few of us negotiate for a living. The

rest of us—a vast majority—must negotiate to get the rest of our jobs done.

- *Win-win is the way.* When both sides win and meet some of their goals, musts, and wants from the negotiation, then the process goes faster, easier, and usually comes out better for everyone. When one side plays to win it all at the other's expense, it creates short-term pain and damages the long-term relationship.

- *Negotiations should be "fast, friendly, and effective."* This favorite phrase should describe most interactions in your business or organization—negotiations and customer relationships in particular. "FFE" works better, takes less time, and produces lasting results and loyalty.

- *The counterparty is not the enemy.* When the counterparty is perceived as the enemy, the negotiation becomes much more negative, antagonistic, personal, and about ego. When you treat someone like an enemy, they do the same, and the win-win mentality is gone forever. I use the term *counterparty*—not *opponent* or *adversary* or similar terms—throughout the book.

- *Negotiations should be for the long term.* At the end of the day, negotiation is about reputation (yours) and relationship (with the counterparty). Doubtless you're going to have to do this again somewhere down the road, and likely with the same counterparty.

HOW THIS BOOK IS ORGANIZED

Negotiating 101 breaks down into six major topics, or parts:

1. Negotiation basics, including the definition and importance of negotiation, are covered in Chapters 1 and 2.
2. Preparation, the "lifeblood of negotiation," is discussed in Chapter 3. The topics covered include but are not limited to research, knowing your counterparties, preparing for the venue, agendas, and visualizing the negotiation from start to finish.
3. Chapters 4 through 6 cover negotiating styles, strategies, tactics, ploys, verbal and nonverbal language, and defenses—both of the prepared beforehand and spontaneous on-stage varieties.
4. Common negotiating pitfalls and how to avoid them are covered in Chapter 7, while using or defending against high-pressure negotiating tactics is the subject of Chapter 8.
5. Chapters 9 and 10 explain how to close and finalize a negotiation. Major elements of creating a contract are also covered.
6. Chapter 11 concludes the book by reinforcing the importance of learning from every negotiation and using it to enhance both your reputation and your long-term relationship, be it with your counterparties or your coworkers and managers.

In the immortal, implied words of most of us who have done it: *Negotiate well and prosper!*

Chapter 1

The Negotiating Imperative

So you think you don't ever have to negotiate? Life just moves forward. In business, negotiating is someone else's job, right? For you, it's just a "discussion." And when you get home from work and have issues to settle with your family, that's just a discussion, too. Right?

Hardly. No matter what you do in today's fast-paced business (and personal) world, every day you'll encounter things you need or want. Not just things, but also behaviors and actions. Discuss them? Yes, it starts with that. But you're not just discussing—you're working out a deal. You're working out an *agreement*.

That agreement can be in the interest of your own individual achievement, your workgroup's achievement, or your organization's achievement as a whole. You want to go get it. That requires negotiation. Especially if you have to give up something—and the other party has to give up something—to reach an agreement.

At its roots, negotiation is the art and science—the process—of getting what you want. This chapter describes further what negotiation is (and isn't), how it fits into today's business and organizational context, and what is (and isn't) new about negotiation today.

WHAT DO WE MEAN BY NEGOTIATION?

What Negotiation Is, What It Means, and Why

Say you run a video production business: Filmographic Productions. Through that business you make some of the best video "shorts" in town. You make excellent local commercials, short training and awareness pieces for business and nonprofit entities, and occasionally some cinema-quality shots for movie producers.

You have two employees and an array of contractors who help out from time to time. You hire actors. Occasionally you hire outside editors. But when someone asks you about your negotiating skills, you laugh. "I don't negotiate," you proclaim.

Think again.

You *do* negotiate. You negotiate with customers over deals and gigs. You negotiate with contractors and employees over duties and price. You negotiate with a landlord. You negotiate with sellers and renters of equipment. You negotiate for the use of props and places to shoot. You negotiate with local police departments to close roads and run traffic breaks. You negotiate for studio time.

You probably spend more time negotiating than shooting film.

You need negotiating skills.

Now suppose, instead of running your own production business, you're an admin specialist at a large company. Your boss and department members you support do most of the "outside" negotiating with customers and suppliers—your job is to support them.

Think you don't need negotiating skills? You bet you do. You have to negotiate for people's time. You have to negotiate for meeting rooms. You have to negotiate with the nighttime janitor to make sure meeting notes aren't erased from the conference room whiteboard. You have to negotiate for your own vacation time and perhaps for your salary and other forms of compensation.

You must negotiate and negotiate well. Not just to perform the duties of the job, but also to avoid losing control of what's going on in your work. A large part of your job is about negotiation. You do it all the time.

And when you log off and go home? Think the negotiating stops there? Hardly. You have to negotiate with the young ones to get their homework done and to be home in time for dinner. You have to negotiate with your partner over everything from who does the dishes to larger decisions like where you're taking the family for vacation next time around.

These examples just touch on negotiations within your inner world—your workplace, your home, your family. The spectrum widens considerably when you consider the negotiations necessary to buy something big or to get your furnace fixed or to get the best deal on a cellular plan.

Every one of us negotiates every day. Not necessarily from sunup to sundown—but a lot. It's an unavoidable feature of today's life.

NEGOTIATION, DEFINED

I always like to begin coverage on an important topic, in this case negotiation, by defining the term itself and giving some insight into what it is and what it isn't. So here are some popular definitions, including one of my own, for the word *negotiation*. I've also made some comments about each:

- *Negotiation is a discussion aimed at reaching an agreement* (Oxford Dictionaries). This is the simplest and most straightforward definition

I could find. End result: an "agreement." Process: a "discussion." The definition captures the basics and is a good place to start, but it doesn't tell us much about the discussion or the agreement.

- *Negotiation is a dialogue between two or more people or parties intended to reach a beneficial outcome* (Wikipedia). Here we get a little more "color" on both the discussion and the agreement. The discussion is between two or more parties; the agreement is a "beneficial outcome." Of course that raises the question, "Beneficial to whom?" I'll come back to that topic, but cutting to the chase for a moment—beneficial to *both* parties (win-win) is usually best.

- *Negotiation is a give and take process between two or more parties, each with its own aims, needs, and viewpoints* (Business Dictionary). Still better. I like "give and take." That's what we do in the discussion—give on some points in order to take on others, back and forth, back and forth, until a satisfactory agreement, hopefully for both parties, is reached. I like the enhanced description of the parties and their interests—each with its own "aims, needs, and viewpoints." True.

- *Negotiation is about having a give and take discussion with other parties, often with opposing interests, to get something important that you want or need or to achieve a goal* (my definition). My somewhat more labored definition covers a lot of ground: "give and take discussion" and "other parties with opposing interests." I added "to get something important"—I feel that this is an important pretext, for it is seldom worth the energy to negotiate for something that *isn't* important (a "tempest in a teapot")—yet it seems that people are disposed to do it all the time! Don't waste time; negotiate when it counts. The outcome should be something you want or need, or to achieve a goal. You should not negotiate for negotiating's sake—again a common downfall. Negotiate smart, not just often!

THE OTHER SIDE OF THE COIN

What Negotiation *Isn't*

Quite often the best way to understand what something *is* is to understand what it *isn't*. In that light it's worth taking a minute to list out a few "isn'ts" about negotiation.

When we hear the word *negotiation*, we might conjure up negative images based on past events. Maybe we recall news broadcasts filled with venomous stories and diatribes about adversarial, ugly, and even vicious negotiations between archrivals. One story might have been about a union pitted against management to end or avert a strike; another story might have been about a negotiation for the release of a hostage. Regardless, stories like these don't exactly make us want to get involved in negotiating something. In fact, most of us would probably wish to distance ourselves as much as possible.

But not all negotiations are venomous, and certainly not all are high-stakes affairs on behalf of unions or hostages or other combative groups. Most negotiations are far tamer than what might occur in these situations.

With that in mind, a well-planned, well-executed negotiation *is not* any of the following:

- *Not a confrontation.* Yes, the two sides may have different views, goals, wants, or needs. But the discussion of those factors should be calm, civil, and factual—not an "I win, you lose" confrontation.
- *Not an argument.* Same idea. Both of you have something to gain from the negotiation.
- *Not a disagreement.* However, the negotiation may play a role in settling a disagreement.

- *Not a shouting match.* Again, peace carries the day. Negotiation brings both sides together rather than driving them apart.
- *Not a win-lose proposition (in most cases).* A win-lose mentality may create more advantage today but loses in the long run as you alienate your counterparty.

A good negotiation is a peaceful, thought-out effort to reach an agreement on something important through well-prepared and executed negotiating skills, strategies, and tactics.

Negotiation—Fear Not!

Because of the perceived confrontational nature of negotiation, many people shy away from it as they would from confrontation itself. Such a fear is natural. But just as the natural fear of public speaking can be overcome, there are ways to overcome the fear of negotiation and even channel that fear into energy to be successful!

Successful public speakers will tell you that the best way to overcome fear in speaking is preparation. Know your stuff, be prepared for the unexpected, and boost your confidence through knowledge. It works every time for speakers, and the same principles apply for negotiators. Be prepared. With enough preparation, no one (your business adversary, your employee, or your teenager) will be able to trip you up.

As John F. Kennedy said in his 1961 presidential inauguration address: "Let us never negotiate out of fear. But let us never fear to negotiate."

NEGOTIATION AND THE FAST TRACK IN BUSINESS

Speed Now More Than Ever

Negotiation is all around us—no matter who you are in the business world—and as noted above, it doesn't stop when you come home from work. Although the primary focus of this book is to help you become a more effective business negotiator, it is always worth keeping in mind that negotiations happen all the time outside of work, and that the same skills and strategies apply.

Negotiation is a basic part of life; this is the reality of today's fast-paced world. Although some might think that the negotiation involved with a project takes away time from managing it, in fact negotiating is *part of* managing the project. For most projects tackled in today's commercial world, negotiation is an increasingly vital part of the process. Why? Let's look into it.

THE NEED FOR SPEED

All this negotiating has to be done faster than ever before. These days, business, technology, and products all move at a blinding speed. So does your competition, and if you don't keep up with them, you'll be left behind. In the case of the video production company I discussed earlier, you'll get a very narrow window of time to negotiate the deal and a limited time to put the production together. You can't spend all your time negotiating. You must get the negotiations done quickly so that you can move on to producing the new product.

Your client has tight deadlines to meet, after all. If negotiations bog down, your clients will begin to look elsewhere and your competition will "get the worm" first!

For this reason most negotiations must occur very quickly—quicker than ever before. Often they are tucked into odd moments of the day as executives and employees tap relentlessly on their smartphones. These days, there is often no time to hold face-to-face meetings with the players involved. Some part, if not all, of the negotiations will probably be done by email, phone, instant messaging (IM), or even text.

The goal of every negotiation is to get what you need or want as quickly as possible so that you and your organization can move forward without delays. However, even at this accelerated pace, you must beware of harmful concessions or oversights—or of missing the boat completely. The price of being slow is high; the price of negotiating poorly can be even higher.

The tactics you employ come from an assortment of traditional negotiating techniques, all sped up to accomplish what ideally is a win-win. But even when the negotiation has been concluded and the terms agreed upon, you're not done. Even when running in fast mode, it's important to come away with what you want, while also preserving a long-term relationship with the other party. Why? Because your hope is that you'll be working with these same people in the future.

Why So Fast Today?

There can be no doubt that in today's world, the speed of business has increased. This isn't just a result of texting, IM, or other communications media.

The changes in the speed of business are a reflection of structural changes in the nature of business and commerce itself. Whereas twenty or thirty years ago it might have taken a long time—several years, possibly—for a product to go from prototype to market, companies today bring products to market far more quickly. Business must respond to a rapidly changing customer base, one that's plugged into the Internet and gets its information at the speed of light. The computer and connectivity technology developed in the late twentieth century has come home to roost, and propels a never-ending wave of innovation and new information.

This creates a snowball effect. Fast requires fast, and pretty soon, everybody is trying to eke out the slightest competitive advantage before the competition gets there. "Publish or perish" is a long-standing epigram in the academic world, and it applies to commercial industry as well. Companies must produce competitive products more swiftly. To maintain their place in the industry, they must go faster, and to go faster, they must *negotiate* faster. It happens everywhere.

So what does that mean for you as a businessperson? You must go faster, too. You must negotiate faster; and you must get it done in a fast, friendly, and effective manner.

If you don't negotiate "fast, friendly, and effective," it only slows down your business later on down the road.

NEGOTIATION AND NEW TECHNOLOGY

Everything Is Faster

The advent of new technology and connectivity has enabled us to communicate more quickly and more effectively than ever before. If you don't use the latest technology devices to negotiate or do business in general, you're likely to be left out of the loop. Technology influences the negotiating playbook in other ways, too, as it:

1. *Enables fast and real-time research.* Technology allows us to instantly look up facts. We can research competitive products and prices, sales channels, product performance, peer reviews, legal or regulatory requirements, market research, and a host of other factors pertinent to a negotiation at the blink of an eye. You can use these research tools in advance and on the day of the show. Have the facts—and know where to get the facts you don't bring with you. Being prepared is not only easier and more important than ever, it is *expected*.
2. *Requires shorter learning curves.* Along with the acquisition of facts, technology devices enable negotiation participants to become experts faster. Not only should you use technology to quickly get up to speed on all the fine points of your negotiation you should also expect that the negotiators on the other side of the table have done the same.
3. *Demands learning how to use new tools.* If you conduct face-to-face negotiation, you'll find that today's technologies are typically well integrated into most negotiation rooms or workplaces.

Additionally, they are excellent tools for sharing visuals or documents if you're negotiating remotely. Learn how to use these tools; otherwise your counterparty will have an edge.

Even Facebook Can Help

As strange as it may seem, even such social media sites as Facebook or LinkedIn can help you with a negotiation if used properly. For instance, you can learn more about your counterparty. Even discovering just a few personal tidbits, such as an obvious interest in water skiing, can give you a platform to break the ice and establish rapport.

Having a handle on professional information of course is always a plus. Knowing someone's professional background can help you size up what she knows and doesn't know, and what she brings into the negotiation.

Further, you can use the Internet to search for public commentary about a product or service, either through a retailer that sells the product (e.g., Amazon) or through a plain search engine search (e.g., "customer comments [product X]"). You'll not only learn what customers think, you're likely to see some professional or journalistic reviews as well.

You'll be surprised what you can learn about people—and products and services—easily and quickly.

YOU'RE ON YOUR OWN!

It's a Do-It-Yourself World

One of the prevailing features of a workplace these days is that—to a large degree because of technology and efficiency improvements—you're on your own now more than ever, to tackle the task of negotiation.

Thirty years ago most of us in any kind of medium or large firm had help to navigate the choppy waters of business. There was a support staff. Secretaries, administrative assistants, sales development people, contracts people, even professional negotiators were in the office or nearby to help us research and develop business deals. We determined what needed to be done, what needed to be researched, what needed to be written, and where the meeting was to be held. Someone else did the legwork.

Now, of course, that's all changed. PCs, networks, email, cell phones, IM, and voicemail have made us all our own secretaries. The Internet has made us our own researchers and meeting arrangers. Companies have cut their support staff to the bone. As a result, these support tasks have been offloaded onto the rest of us. Corporate hierarchies, while they still exist, are easily transcended by electronic communication.

What does that mean? It means that in most circumstances you've become your own negotiator.

NEGOTIATION—IT'S EVERYWHERE

Not only must we do our own negotiating, but negotiating has become a way of life for most of us. We negotiate for our existing projects. We negotiate for new jobs, new projects, raises, flexible work schedules, and travel arrangements. We negotiate with workplace individuals and departments, and with individuals and organizations on the outside. Rare is a day when you aren't in some kind of negotiation, either with an employee or direct supervisor or with someone external to your company.

Much of the bargaining we do is with people we seldom or never had to negotiate with before. Negotiation has replaced a hierarchical order that was once much more dominant in families and in our personal lives. In today's world, we have to negotiate with our children. We have to negotiate with our schools. We have to negotiate with various players in our personal financial lives, including other members of the family.

Of course, not only are there more issues to negotiate, but these negotiations are all going faster. Your teenagers will negotiate with you (though it may not seem like a negotiation) over their cell phone. They'll send you a link minutes beforehand showing you the car they want to buy, and God help you if you don't look at it before you talk. You negotiate who's picking them up, and when.

You're busy, so you've contracted home services—housekeeping, yard maintenance, and so on. There's another negotiation. Is your mother coming for a visit today or tomorrow? There's another negotiation. You'd better check the weather. Prepare (if you can), and respond now.

Not only is there more to negotiate, and not only does it all go faster, but everything changes faster, too. New information arrives faster and is easier to get. The shipment will be late? Renegotiate the project due date, and renegotiate people's time and availability. Price change? Gotta deal with that. Kid just got invited to a friend's house via a text message? Negotiate that deal (probably also by text).

The bottom line: If you're like most people, you spend most of your time these days working out some kind of arrangement with someone. It's a connected world. Because those connections are electronic, they operate in real time. To cope in this world, you need to negotiate in real time as well, and you need to do it efficiently.

THE DIFFERENCE BETWEEN NEGOTIATING AND SELLING

Yes, There Is a Difference

You're new to the idea of negotiating. You were hired into your organization as an engineer, a technical expert. You had years of education to acquire a technical credential, because you didn't see yourself as a salesperson. But now you've been invited into a negotiation to sell your product to an eager customer. You think to yourself, "How did I get here? I chose a career path deliberately to avoid becoming a salesperson. Sales is not what I'm good at, so why am I here?"

The point—and you probably saw this coming—is that you *aren't* selling. You're *negotiating*. What's the difference?

Simply put: Selling is the act of persuading someone to buy your product or idea, while negotiating is the act of working out the details of the deal.

In some situations you'll see a clear transition from one phase to the other, but in many you won't. As the engineer on the team, you may be involved in the late stages of selling by providing some technical detail, but it's more likely you'll be called on to help with details in the negotiation itself.

A good negotiation occurs after the sale is made; it doesn't backtrack into the selling phase. However, as you undoubtedly know, that's not how things work in the real world. In many cases the counterparty will arrive unsure, or at least act that way as a bargaining ploy.

If your company executives told you that you'd never be involved in selling, they probably lied. But if you focus on the negotiating part of the deal—and recognize the difference between negotiating and selling—you'll be more effective as a team member and happier with your role.

NEGOTIATING PROFESSIONALS AND PROFESSIONAL NEGOTIATORS

A *professional negotiator* is someone who specializes in negotiating; 80 to 90 percent of his job is to prepare for and conduct negotiations on a company's or client's behalf. He is a specialist well versed and experienced in the strategies and tactics of negotiation. He is a "hired gun," usually more trained and experienced in the process of negotiating than the business, product, or service itself.

A *negotiating professional* is someone who has a full-time job in an organization doing a task or function, such as product marketing, product development, product support, accounting, or some such. These people may be called into a formal negotiation, and of course they will do many smaller negotiations throughout the day on everything from a product price decision to the size of their cubicle in a new floor layout. They negotiate, but their negotiation skillset and experience are only adjacent to their main duties and function.

With the negotiating imperative and today's negotiating context in mind, the next few chapters give an overview of negotiation basics, followed by strategies, tactics, and "day of show" techniques designed to make you a better negotiator regardless of the context or speed of the negotiation. Some things have changed, and some have stayed the same. What follows examines both.

Chapter 2

Negotiation—The Basics

Perhaps you haven't realized it, but you've been playing the negotiating game all your life. You were doing it as a child, then as an adolescent. You negotiated with your parents over free time, homework time, and dinnertime. You negotiated with your friends over swapping lunches at school, or who got to pitch and who got to bat in your street baseball games. You kept it up as an adult. These days you negotiate "business-to-consumer" to buy a car or a mobile phone or a vacation package. You negotiate "consumer-to-consumer" to buy or sell stuff on Craigslist or eBay. And at work you conduct "business-to-business" negotiations.

All through this, consciously or subconsciously, you've been developing core negotiating skills and experiences. No matter who you are or where you came from, you have played the negotiating game. You may be better at this than you think.

While those days of negotiating for baseball cards or dollhouse furniture may have long faded into history, the practice and promise of negotiating has most likely stayed with you. And it has probably become more important than ever in the life you lead today. This chapter is designed to connect your innate negotiating skills with a few basics on how today's negotiating game is played. The idea is to put some structure around what you already do. Subsequent chapters will help you build upon that basic structure so that you can round out your negotiating skillset.

THE HISTORY OF NEGOTIATION

From Bartering to the Conference Table

Where, how, when, and why did negotiation become a part of civilized society? It really started as barter—the direct exchange of goods or services with no money or other intermediary item of value involved.

When the first barter in human history took place is unknown, but we do know that bartering has been around for much longer than buying and selling. It grew up as a system of give-and-take that accommodated anyone who chose to participate. Whether it was to acquire a chunk of lamb in exchange for some pottery or to obtain jewelry for a hand-painted headpiece, people found ways to fulfill their needs.

Bartering is an exchange of goods or services without the use of money as an item of value or as an equalizer in the transaction. The worth of the objects or services being exchanged is up to the two parties involved, and a negotiation is how the two parties establish worth. That negotiation in early history, as in today's negotiations, could happen very quickly or over the course of days, depending on the degree of difference between the two negotiating parties, the size and importance of the deal, and the willingness of the parties to work to find the best deal (which correlates directly to its importance).

Bartering was a way to acquire life's necessities, but it was more than that—it broke down the barriers of communication. When people met for the first time, bartering was a way to determine who was trustworthy and genuine, and only after mutual willingness to trade was expressed would a dialogue between the two parties ensue. (This is equally true today, particularly when so much of our interaction occurs in cyberspace.)

Bartering slowly evolved into a primitive financial arrangement, in which cows, sheep, and other livestock were used as forms of currency. Plants, produce, and other agricultural items also served as currency, only to be overtaken by precious metals, stones, and finally paper bills.

When Money Appeared on the Scene

Cowries—marine snails boasting thick, glossy shells peppered with tiny flecks—were used in China in 1200 B.C.E. as the first money. They were widely used, and even became popular in faraway places such as Africa, where some cultures continue to exchange them today. Cowries are the longest-used currency in history. In this modern era of real-time foreign exchange quotes, we still have no idea how many cowries there are to a dollar. However, as should be obvious from a swift scan of the financial news, today's economy is powered by money, and money is by far the most important element of exchange. While most of today's money is electronic—that is, it exists as a bank or some other kind of electronic balance rather than physical (paper bills and coins)—it still serves the same purpose: to facilitate exchange.

FROM BARTERING TO NEGOTIATING

When people bartered, most of the time they knew the values of the objects they exchanged. Suppose that three baskets of corn were generally worth one chicken. Two parties had to persuade each other to execute the exchange, but they didn't have to worry about setting the price. But what if one year there was a drought and there wasn't much corn to go around? Then a farmer with three baskets of corn could perhaps bargain to exchange them for two or even three chickens. Bargaining the exchange value of something is a form of negotiating. It works once you switch to a currency system—you simply negotiate the value of something in exchange for a specific dollar or other currency value.

As primitive as this sounds, most likely you've seen it in person. The way people bargain with each other varies from culture to culture, but you've no doubt seen bargaining take place at a yard sale or flea market. The vendor gives you a price, you give the vendor a price, and eventually either a happy medium is decided upon or you walk away. More often than not, the vendor inches down on her price while you inch up on your price, until you're both at a number that doesn't allow either one of you to budge any further.

A different type of bargaining can be seen at an auction, where a roomful of people view the items up for sale and make their bids on the items they wish to buy. Someone makes a bid on an item. Another person makes a higher bid. Another jumps in to make yet a higher bid. This bidding continues back and forth until one person has outbid all interested parties. Today, millions of people search for, post, trade, barter, bid, and buy anything from toys they had as children to signed sports paraphernalia on eBay and other Internet auction sites. If only our sheep-trading ancestors could see us now!

Bargaining Is about Price

If all we did was barter, we probably wouldn't need a whole book to discuss the nature of negotiating. Whether three baskets of corn was worth one or two chickens is more a matter of the prevailing "market" at the time than the negotiating technique employed. So what has happened to good old-fashioned bartering that merits a fancier word—and dozens of books like this one on the topic of negotiating?

The difference between *bartering*, or *bargaining*, and *negotiating* boils down to complexity and process. While the terms *bargaining* and *negotiating* seem synonymous, there's a difference between the two.

Bargaining, which is today's equivalent to bartering but typically incorporates money, involves streamlining wants and needs into a single focus. Before you ever step foot into your neighbor's yard sale, you well know that all the handwritten sticker prices are not permanent. Your goal is to get the item you desire at the lowest possible price. Your neighbor's goal on the other hand is twofold—to get rid of as many items as possible and to get the most amount of money possible for them.

When it comes to bargaining, it's all about price. Both parties focus on trying to get the best deal for themselves. In this case, money is the focal point, and that's when the price war begins: "How much?" "A dollar." "I'll give you fifty cents." "Eighty cents." "Sixty cents." "Seventy cents." "Sixty-five cents." "Deal."

When a goal becomes concentrated, it's easy to lose sight of all the things that could be important in the discussion. In the yard sale example, price takes precedence over the usefulness of the product. The purchaser never stops to think, "If I thought it was worth only fifty cents a minute ago, why do I think it's worth more now?" Although the settled price was split equally down the middle, one person spent more than she intended to and the other person received less money for the item than he hoped to receive. So who got the bargain? Both did, in a way—the buyer still paid less than full price while the seller got more than the buyer's original offer.

Some people are said to "drive a hard bargain," meaning there's little to no chance of swaying them away from believing their offer is fair. You can't bargain with them—they are convinced that they know best or that there's someone out there who'll pay the full price. Thus, the department-store mentality is born, and the only way you're ever paying a lower price is if there's a sale.

Negotiating Is about the "Whole" Deal

Negotiating, on the other hand, is about getting agreement or settling a question between two parties. It's not always about price, and even when price is involved the negotiation usually isn't *limited* to price. Negotiating takes in all attributes of a deal. Delivery, timing, extras, the right to negotiate a future deal, a *relationship* all are likely to be included—and in many cases, there's no financial transaction involved at all.

THE NEGOTIATING GAME

Strategies and Tactics

Negotiating, as we defined in Chapter 1, is about getting something important that you want or need. It is about achieving a goal through a give-and-take discussion with two or more parties. It can easily be seen as a "game" (with a desired outcome and a series of strategies and tactics) and "moves" (deployed consecutively to get to that outcome).

A negotiation has a beginning, a middle, and a finish, with a strategy and desired outcome envisioned beforehand. Parties can and do make day-of-the-game course corrections, adjustments, and other changes to accommodate the moves of the counterparty as they occur. In contrast to bargaining, the outcome in a negotiation is usually multidimensional—as are the strategies and tactics you deploy to get there.

Like a game of chess, in a negotiation there are many possible intermediate positions you can reach to get to the ultimate goal. Your success depends on how you go about achieving those positions and responding to your counterparty's moves—as you don't control everything. However, because there are multidimensional goals and negotiating points, in many ways a business negotiation is more complex and involved than a game of chess. As well, there are far more interpersonal and human aspects to most negotiations.

Not a Chess Player? Nothing to Fear!

You'll do well to think of negotiating as a game, like a chess game, as you approach it. But again, unlike and beyond chess, it is often not about how well you calculate that determines the outcome, but how well you communicate and work with your counterparty. It's about how you satisfy your counterparty's needs while also taking care of your own. Unlike chess, it is often possible and always desirable to get the counterparty on your side, to work effectively and amicably with your counterparty. So those of you who shy away from the hard, cold calculations of a chess game—there's hope! In a negotiation, those of you with good interpersonal skills will almost always outplay the calculating chess player!

POSITIONAL AND WIN-WIN NEGOTIATION

Although several forms of negotiation will be discussed in this book, the two most common are positional negotiating and win-win negotiating. Particularly in today's fast-paced and heavily interconnected world, of these two types of negotiation you should embrace win-win negotiation as the more useful approach.

Positional Negotiation

Positional negotiating occurs when each side takes a position and is hesitant to yield, or yield much, to the other. Each side is committed to its course of action—hopefully, but not always, for a business reason. Business reasons can mean things like budget or cost constraints, design constraints, specific customer needs that must be met, and so forth. Note that the party "digging in" has a business rationale for doing so.

But often—too often, really—one side takes, and tries to keep, a tough position for personal reasons: ego, a "win-at-all-costs" or "win-lose" mentality, sheer habit, or even sometimes just because they took and held a particular position successfully last time around. You should always avoid the temptation to take and hold a position in a positional negotiation for personal reasons—always ask yourself: "Is there a business reason why I'm doing this?"

At the same time, you should learn to recognize counterproductive positional negotiation tendencies in your counterparty. You may know about these tendencies before they walk into the room, or you may learn about them in the early moments of the negotiation. You'll have to think quickly once you determine that this style is in play. You can then either "fight fire with fire" or perhaps, more effectively, reach across the table and suggest that you both could accomplish a lot more, and do so faster, if both sides collaborated on a win-win.

Win Now May Mean Lose Later

You may win a few negotiations in the short term with a steadfast winner-take-all positional strategy. But you're likely to lose in the long term, as it takes more time and energy. And your opponents will be forced to negotiate to win as well—throwing a possible win-win out the window.

In positional negotiations, both sides become so focused on their own needs that they fail to comprehend those of the other party. A power struggle often ensues and the parties never really get around to discussing their goals and objectives. As a result hours are wasted trying to produce agreements that everyone can get behind. In addition, the negativity and struggle can jeopardize long-term relationships and make the negotiation that much harder.

In short: don't be a "tough guy." It only makes things harder, and in today's competitive environment, your counterparties may simply walk.

Win-Win Negotiation

Instead of positional negotiation, which is really win-lose in the end, you can—and should—try to engage in a win-win style and strategy. Win-win means that both parties come away satisfied such that their needs, or at least *most* of their needs, are addressed and met. When both sides come away with items they want and need, agreements are made more easily, take less time, and preserve or even enhance the long-term relationship between parties—important in business as well as in personal situations.

Being successful at win-win negotiating means getting good at understanding and anticipating your counterparty's needs; it also means being a bit more flexible with your own needs and wants in order to hammer out the collaborative solution. Playing fair—being up front and honest about your needs and your responses to theirs—is also important.

Win-win negotiating is successful because everyone goes into the process with a positive attitude, a firm understanding of how the game is played, and a professional approach to the situation at hand. Such an approach begets trust, and where there is trust, more and better results quickly follow.

In most cases, the successful negotiation starts with a win-win end in mind. Ultimately, win-win negotiation is almost always a gratifying way to do business. It should be no surprise that much of the remainder of this book is constructed around the idea of win-win negotiation.

Concessions: The Essential Tool of the Win-Win Negotiation

You go to the bakery department at your grocery store. You're looking for four dinner rolls, but your grocery bakery only carries packages of eight dinner rolls. What to do? You might ask the clerk to take four out of the bag and price them accordingly. In these situations you're asking the company you regularly do business with for a *concession*. What you offer in return is your continued business and a positive opinion about the company's services.

What is a concession? A concession is when you yield to a counterparty's needs by giving him or her a privilege not usually given to other people. For example, during a business meeting, an executive asks for a 10 percent cut in production costs. The other executive agrees to this concession, but she asks for one of her own in return—to be able to hire or contract in a few more employees. In today's rapid negotiating climate, concessions can also be made in the interest of time. For example, you might agree to pay a higher price or accept slower delivery if the counterparty waives certain approval requirements so as to finish the negotiation more quickly.

WHEN THEY DON'T WANT TO PLAY

Find the Reason

You want to make a deal to pave your parking lot or fix the roof on your building or procure 5,000 custom integrated circuits to build into your product. You reach out to contact your favorite supplier, but he doesn't return your phone call right away. You wait a few days. He doesn't return your phone call at all. You think your need and the business deal is pretty straightforward, and you think you have a pretty good relationship with these suppliers and contractors. So what's going on?

The first step is to simply find out why. Follow up with a phone call, leave a message if necessary simply asking why they aren't prepared to negotiate with you. There may be a simple explanation. Maybe the counterparty doesn't have the time to do the work or even negotiate just yet but would be willing to work with you at a later date.

If the reason why remains elusive, find out the "what" or "how." What can you put forth in order to make your request to negotiate more attractive? What can you put forth to make the negotiation quicker or easier? Can you throw some other business their way to make it more attractive? Can you be flexible with deadlines or project staging to allow the counterparty to work in other projects? If you can, you're likely to get a better deal. If you can't, you may stir up the stinging bees of a positional negotiation—or just as bad, continue to be ignored altogether.

Bottom line: it doesn't hurt to make or suggest a few concessions right in the beginning. You want to get the counterparty to the table, and you want to get them to the table feeling positive.

SEPARATING THE PEOPLE
FROM THE PROBLEM

Suppose you're just getting started on what might be a tense negotiation with a state regulatory agency on environmental compliance concerning your business. Your dander is up. This isn't going to be good, you can feel it. And your negotiating partner is already writing off the counterparty as a "bunch of tree-huggers who don't deserve the time of day." You've met with this team before, and their body language among other things reflected that they may not just feel so good about you guys, either.

Is this negotiation likely to get off on the right foot? Are you going to be able to stick to the facts and issues? Will you be able to stay on task? Are you likely to be successful at hammering out a win-win solution quickly while also building a long-term trusting relationship?

Probably not, unless you can separate the people from the problem and deal with each in its own sphere.

One of the core principles pervasive to the practice of effective negotiation is the idea of separating the people—the personal emotions, perceptions, and biases inherent in a negotiation (because negotiations are done by people!)—from the real issues being discussed.

Here are a few techniques for dealing with the people issues and keeping them from sundering your win-win problem-solving efforts:

1. *Put your (negative) perceptions in check.* Sure, the environmental agency negotiators don't "live in the real world" of running a business. But don't assume that they aren't aware of what that real world is all about. If your negative perceptions turn out to be right—that they are insensitive about the needs of your

business—take a short time-out to give them an objective and factual overview of what you do and how the environmental regulations make that painful.

2. *Realize that they probably want the same thing you do.* At the end of the day they want a solution too, and they want it quickly. They don't want to have to put excessive time and energy into the case, and they probably don't want to deal with your people issues any more than they have to! They would like to walk away with a deal and a relationship.

3. *Practice empathy.* The counterparty's negotiators are people too, trying to be successful in achieving their goals without too much pain and suffering. They have families to support and other work to do, just like you do. They have a job to get done. Respect that and help them do it, and they'll do the same.

4. *Take time-outs.* When basketball coaches sense things are becoming too emotional and personal, they call a time-out to take players' minds off the game at hand. You can—and should—do this, too. If you sense tension or interpersonal conflict, don't let it overheat. Instead, take a break so that everyone can cool off. Better yet, use the break time to discuss some common ground topic like your recent vacations or the new city recreation center. Whatever the topic, the goal is to establish rapport and reinforce the fact that you're both "human."

5. *Keep communications effective.* Listen actively, and talk when it's your turn. Don't use harsh or bullying language, and don't react or respond to theirs. While you might put them on the defensive insofar as your problem is concerned, don't put them on the defensive personally. Never talk down to anyone, and if they talk down to you, just ignore it.

What it comes down to is this: Always think positive and realize that the proverbial glass is half full when it comes to working with people. When you can do that successfully, you'll put the personal conflicts aside and free up your team—both teams, really—to deal more effectively with the problem.

Again, Negotiating Is Everywhere

Put simply, everyone negotiates. Parents negotiate with teachers; husbands negotiate with wives; brothers negotiate with sisters; defense attorneys negotiate with prosecuting attorneys; and so forth. Even children exercise a form of negotiating. It's funny how adults are still playing the game of "I'll trade you this for that" albeit in a more sophisticated and refined manner.

While you may play down these personal-life negotiations, if you're in any kind of business or professional environment, you probably negotiate a lot. Deals are done, budgets are created, and money is spent or acquired through negotiation. Bridges are built, roads are repaired, high-rises are erected, public transportation is rerouted, and streets are named—and all the while, there's a group of professionals negotiating the details of these projects by presenting their ideas and strategies to the appropriate approving manager, approval committee, or board of directors. You may be finding yourself vying for a multimillion-dollar deal for your business—or for a $150 admission ticket to a trade show you'd like to attend. Both are negotiations, and both require much of the same set of skills.

In sum, negotiating is about getting what you want. Win-win negotiating is about getting what you want through the recognition of your goals and the goals of a counterparty, and finding a peaceful solution that sends everyone away with maximum satisfaction with minimal time consumed. In today's rapidly moving world, time is of the essence. Luckily, the real-time information available at our fingertips helps us find that win-win more quickly and precisely than ever before.

Chapter 3

Getting Started: Preparation, Preparation, and More Preparation

Public speakers say that the secret to success is preparation. Their advice: "Prepare one hour for every minute of the speech." Why? Not only to know the material but also to build confidence. You benefit when you channel all that loose energy and nervousness into confidence. And then when you deliver your speech you appear "better" than the audience because you know your stuff.

It works. And such a mantra is easily ported over to the world of negotiation. Be prepared and you'll know your stuff. Moreover, you'll come off as though you know your stuff, which is important in gaining the respect and collaboration of your counterparties.

This can't be stressed enough: prepare, prepare and prepare. That's what this chapter's about—what, how, and when to prepare for a negotiation.

PREPARING THE GROUND

Getting Ready for the Game

I've described negotiation as a game. There are rules, but beyond the rules are strategies and tactics to achieve your goals and do something important. Like any game, winning is the ultimate goal; that's why you enter the negotiation in the first place. But unlike most games, we like to see the counterparty win too—a win-win. That's not the primary goal of a negotiation, but it's an important *strategy*. Letting the counterparty win too is a strategy that helps us get what we want, and it's a strategy that helps everyone get through the negotiation more quickly.

But win-win isn't the only strategy, and it doesn't begin to cover the topic of tactics. As the saying goes, the "devil is in the details." You must not only know your stuff but, like a good game-player, you must also be able to envision your moves—sometimes several moves in advance—to keep the game going your way. Like any game, it works best to have an all-inclusive understanding of the game so that you can be aware of what's going on and gain and preserve your advantage.

This in turn requires preparation. It's not just about the rules of the game per se. It's about developing a thorough understanding of the question at hand, the topic of the negotiation. It's about knowing the facts, understanding the nuanced "gray areas" and unknowns around the facts, understanding your team, understanding your counterparty, and even being familiar with the very "ground" or venue in which the negotiation will occur. Any shortfall in preparation in any of these areas can create awkwardness—which in turn may create weaknesses your opponent can exploit.

KNOW YOURSELF AND YOUR GOALS

Before doing any research into the facts, figures, and dynamics of a negotiation, it's important to *visualize* what you want out of the negotiation. If you're negotiating for a bridge construction contract, you may have a dollar figure in mind, with associated construction times, crew deployments, and other details to go with it. If you're negotiating with your fifteen-year-old about cleaning up his own dishes, you want to achieve that outcome, but you want to do it in a positive, nurturing way—no hard feelings. Sizing up these "musts" and "wants" all works toward setting goals, which in turn becomes a framework for the negotiation.

Start with the End in Mind

The essence is "seeing" the outcome. Try to imagine what a finished deal will look like, then work backward through the negotiation process, the back and forth, the give and take, all the way to the facts and information you'll bring into the negotiation. Of course, you can't visualize everything, but the vision will help you organize your thoughts and be better prepared to cover the gaps—the unknowns—when they come into view.

Organizing your thoughts around a vision of the negotiation will give both your research and your day-of-show performance some direction and purpose. It provides focus. It's always better to start with something rather than nothing, and the more you have in hand through preparation, the easier the task, the smoother the process, and the more likely you'll achieve the outcome you want—the end goal you visualized in the first place.

In contrast, if you walk into a negotiation unprepared, unsure, and undecided on what you hope to achieve, the counterparty—especially if a seasoned negotiator—will seize upon this opportunity to dominate the negotiation and make it all about her needs. Additionally, because you're unsure about the facts or the final outcome you want, you'll be unarmed in the face of the many concessions likely to be demanded of you.

Visualizing the Outcome

To help determine the "end in mind" you want, you might start setting goals and strategies by asking yourself the following questions:

- What do I hope to achieve in the negotiation?
- What is my main goal? The *best* outcome?
- What are my secondary goals?
- What are my "musts" and "wants"?
- What can prevent me from being successful?
- What are the likely specific stumbling blocks?
- How can I overcome these stumbling blocks?
- What preparatory steps can I take to make the negotiation quick and successful?

Obviously these questions are at a very general level and can be modified according to the specifics of the negotiation. But they're a good place to start.

Even the simplest of negotiations, like that with your adolescent son over doing his dishes, merit this treatment in part. Think it through. What are your goals and desired outcomes? What will get in the way of a successful negotiation? What are the likely stumbling blocks? Even for such a five-minute (or less!) negotiation, this thought process can help a lot.

About Setting Goals—Keep It Real

Set realistic goals. If a goal is too far out of reach, you'll feel as if you failed if you don't accomplish it, when in reality the goal just wasn't attainable. A goal too far out of reach prevents the win-win. Why? Because your opponent can't come up with anything good enough for your side without compromising his own position. It's also important to be as specific as possible with your goals so that you can track progress toward achieving them.

KNOW YOUR MUSTS AND WANTS

An All-Important Checklist

Almost every negotiation will have a primary goal or goals, and secondary goals. Primary, or main, goals represent the main item(s) you want to accomplish or achieve in the negotiation; secondary goals, which are usually many in number, are just that—important but not as important as the main goal. Often they are attributes of the item being negotiated as the main goal.

Your main goal should be the driving force behind your negotiating position. If you want to buy a car because you need a way to get to work every morning, your main goal is to buy a reliable vehicle. Secondary goals will concern comfort, features, appearance, and price. The means to achieve those goals include the choice of brand, style, model, new versus used, and financing. Within this set of goals you'll be able to prioritize which is most important, check them against the means and possible stumbling blocks, and use the means and anticipated stumbling blocks to ask for concessions and/ or to reprioritize or reshape the goals.

For example, if you prefer a blue car, that becomes a secondary goal. It may be an important one—a "must"—or it may be a "want." That priority, along with your priority for the other goals, helps you know the *value* of that goal toward your outcome. If it's a less important "want" it adds less value to the potential outcome and thus is something to worry less about. You should prepare to give up less-important wants as part of your overall negotiating strategy. If it's a "must" or a very strong "want," then you need to prepare for what you might give up for it.

This seems kind of obvious, but I've seen negotiators break down completely over something that isn't really that important in the grand scheme of the negotiation. They wanted a blue car, but was it worth giving up a deal on a fantastic low-mileage cream puff to attain? In the end, no. But with the wrong perspective going in, a negotiation can easily come off the rails or worse, get you a deal you really don't want.

"See" the Deal Before You Seal the Deal

If you go into the car negotiation dead set on a blue car, you may not be "seeing" how the deal might unfold. If you're stuck on one outcome, that can put you at a disadvantage. Instead, articulate your musts and wants, but don't assume anything going into the negotiation.

VISUALIZE THE NEGOTIATION

I've touched on this already—the idea of "seeing" the end result of the deal; the idea of starting with the end in mind. Now I extend that into the negotiation itself. Here, you attempt to form a mental picture of what will actually happen *during* the negotiation.

If you envision how the meeting will unfold, you can better prepare for situations that might arise; and you can be better prepared to respond to them. If you let your imagination run, you can visualize what might happen and how you'll respond. Sparking the creative side of your brain even before the preparation stage gives you the opportunity to get ready for the unexpected by developing a myriad of protective strategies. For instance, if you visualize that your counterparty might bring experts into the negotiation, you can plan to counter that move.

KNOW YOUR LIMITATIONS AND WEAKNESSES

Given half a glass of water on the table, some of us naturally see it as half full, some of us as half empty. Negotiating thrives on confidence—the ability to be positive, steady, strong, and sure about your subject because you're well prepared—seeing the glass half full. But part of the preparation for the negotiation is also knowing your weak (empty) spots and limitations.

As you visualize the negotiation, you should take inventory on what parts of the deal might be hard for you to deliver on or accept. We've all been there, trying to buy airline tickets three days before we want to travel while still trying to get a low fare. That short notice puts us in a weak negotiating position, but it doesn't mean all is lost; there may be last minute deals available.

Good negotiators are aware of where the weak points are and either try to keep them out of the negotiation altogether or try to downplay their importance. They also look for alternatives: "Sir, I know my shop is backed up with work and I can't produce those stitched-logo T-shirts by next Monday, but how about Tuesday? Or how about a screen printed version?" The weakness of the supplier, of course, is his inability to deliver in the time frame the counterparty wants; the alternatives that the supplier provides are his attempt to get the deal back on track. Notice that he hasn't offered a price concession—yet.

Limitations—How Far You Will or Won't Go

Just like at an auction, it's easy to get caught up in the emotional frenzy of a negotiation and agree to something you wouldn't have without the pressures of the moment. It's human nature, and we've all experienced it. You may have gone into a negotiation prepared to spend no more than $10,000 for a car, but come away spending $10,500 because you found one with exactly what you wanted and couldn't pass it up. If you have the extra $500, no big deal. But it might also break your budget, causing no amount of embarrassment, not to mention concessions on your side, when you are forced to backtrack.

The right approach is to set limitations—minimums, maximums—before you enter the negotiation. Some of those, like goals, are "must" or absolute limitations; some are goals but are not absolute. "I cannot spend over $10,000" is an absolute; whereas "I really don't want a white or silver car" suggests you'll take one if the deal is right.

Limitations set in advance can help prevent the counterparty from discovering your weaknesses. If you know that stitched-logo T-shirts cannot be produced in less than three days, and you are prepared to communicate that during the negotiation, then the counterparty may never find out that the real reason you can't deliver in one day per their request is that your shop is backed up with orders.

Set limitations before you go in—and make sure everyone on your team knows and understands them.

Don't Reveal Weaknesses!

Don't let the other party know what your limitations are—at least not right away. Making your counterparty privy to this information up front might make you seem confrontational and uncompromising. If you absolutely, positively won't spend more than $10,000 on that car, you might not want to disclose that right off, for you might miss out on a really great $10,200 car or another concession the salesperson might make. However, if the counterparty is coming dangerously close to your limits, feel free to say that you don't plan to compromise or go any further on those particular issues.

PLANNING FOR AND USING CONCESSIONS

When to Give a Little Ground

Part of the preparation and visualization process of a negotiation is to get an idea of those points your counterparty might ask for that you're prepared to give some ground on. Typically these are "wants" not "musts," or are tangential details about the main item in question.

As you're visualizing the negotiation, keep in mind that the ability to be flexible may serve to your advantage at some point during the negotiation. While you don't want to easily give up any of your goals or compromise on your limitations, you do want to keep an open mind about how you can adjust your negotiating points if it means a mutual agreement can be reached.

Concessions can be used as adjustments to the negotiation. Concessions are small gives and takes to help both parties arrive at the best win-win solution; they are *refinements* to the deal. You could consider them as tiny "chits" or "perks" to be rationed wisely. They may be asked for and offered in exchange for one another throughout the negotiation. Each party wants to walk out of the room feeling satisfied with the concessions agreed upon. If you did your homework—researched, prepared, practiced, and weighed alternatives—you should have a good idea of what concessions you're comfortable making—and which ones you're comfortable asking for.

CONCESSION STRATEGIES AND TACTICS

When planning and making concessions, here are a few strategic and tactical guidelines to keep in mind:

- *Sequence is important.* If you anticipate multiple concessions, present them in order from least to most important. Getting the easy ones out of the way first may (1) allow you to satisfy your counterparty with only those "easy" ones and (2) allow you to direct the bulk of your time and energy to more important ones.
- *When you present concessions, do so with equal emphasis.* Exhibit the same amount of resistance for every concession so the other party can't tell which have more value to you.
- *For every concession you make, ask for one in return.* For example, "I'll give you a discount if you make a higher down payment."
- *Provide reasons for your requested concessions so the counterparty can understand why you're asking for them.* For example, "I'd like a discount on the sticker price so that I'm able to afford the monthly payments." You'll earn the other party's respect if you prove you're not asking for something just to see if you can get it.

Some experts believe you should always make the first concession. By taking the initiative this way, you retain control over the ones most important to you. Other experts feel that letting the other party make the first concession allows you to take the prize if they overbid. Eventually, you'll develop your own style of negotiating, but for now go with what feels most comfortable to you. Tactics such as these (and many more) will be discussed later in this book.

Remember: Small Successes
Are Still Successes

As you prepare always remember that you can't hit a home run every time you're up at the plate. All good negotiators know that, and all good negotiators know that a lot of singles—small wins—can add up to a big win over time. So if your negotiating position isn't rock solid, you might still be able to achieve a lot of smaller successes, many of the musts and wants on your list, without getting everything. That's how the game works. Get the exact car you want, but for $500 bucks over your "goal" price. Not a bad day, for most folks.

Martin Luther King Jr. said it best: "If I cannot do great things, I can do small things in a great way."

KNOW YOUR COUNTERPARTY

Who They Are, What They Need, How They Operate

Experienced public speakers will emphatically tell you one of the most important elements of the preparation process is *knowing and understanding the audience.*

Why? It's simple. If you know the audience, you can know better what they are looking for, what they need from your pitch, and what questions they're likely to ask. If you're giving a talk on educational opportunities to a group of environmentalists, don't you think they're going to want to know more about the environmental courses you plan to offer? Of course they will.

Your counterparty, like you, will enter the negotiation with his own list of goals, musts, and wants. If you know him, you'll be better prepared to address those musts and wants. There should be fewer—maybe no—surprises.

I can't sufficiently underscore enough the importance of knowing your counterparty before you get started.

KNOWING THEM PROFESSIONALLY AND PERSONALLY

There are two dimensions (usually) to knowing a counterparty. First, you should try to know them as an *organization*—what is their business, what do they offer, what are their strengths and weaknesses, what makes them successful, or not. Second, you should get to know the people within the counterparty—who are they, what role do they serve in their organization, what sort of negotiating style do they use.

Researching the Organization

You can do research on the organization in many ways:

- *Online research.* A quick tour through the organization's website will give you a good idea of their products and how they position them—price, quality, service—and how they do business with their customers.
- *Talk to customers.* If you have the same customers, or you have "peer" customers in your own business, don't hesitate to ask them for more info and the "scoop." If you run a corner deli and are negotiating with a food-service supplier, ask another restaurant-operating peer for his impressions about that supplier.
- *Walk in the door—figuratively or literally.* Prior to the negotiation, pay a visit in person to get a feel for how the counterparty operates. If you're negotiating for a paving project, drop in on one of the others they have in progress. See how they work, what they do. If someone's available, ask questions.

These methods may give you tangible negotiating points or simply give you a better feel for who (as an organization) you're negotiating with.

Researching the People

Your underlying negotiating strategy should be cut to fit the strategy and style of your negotiating opponent. If you've seen your counterparty before as an individual, study her playing style, and learn as much as possible about why she's investing her time in the negotiation. By reviewing the other party's training, accomplishments, education, and work history, for example, you can better predict her actions and be more prepared to address them.

Try to get the specifics of what the other party's goals are early on—so you can weigh your leverage against hers and adjust your game plan if you need to. You can use the first few minutes of the meeting to discuss some of the objectives you share and those that you do not.

Learn as much as you can about the other party's background. What is this person's title? Role in the organization? Experience? What kinds of deals does she negotiate? What is her negotiating style?

In today's split-second information age, it's possible to find out more about people more quickly than ever before. Google, Facebook, LinkedIn, plus the varied ways to network on your own, give you access to information on your counterparty. You can learn a lot about the character of an individual and an organization just by looking around on the web and by tapping into the network.

Always Keep Tabs on the Competition

It almost goes without saying in today's business world—and especially today's negotiating world—that knowing what the competition does and is up to is a vital part of preparation for any negotiation. Simply put—what does the competition do? What concessions do they make and where do they hold firm?

In today's information age, it is possible to research negotiating points and concessions very quickly and easily online. But you might also want to deploy a little "shoe leather"—get out and research in person. If you run a restaurant, have a meal at the competition's once in a while (you're probably tired of eating your own cooking anyhow!).

Find out what your competitors offer—price, service, and intangibles—and how each compares to your own product or service. Understand your counterparty's competition as well—this may even be more important. If you're selling packaging materials to an electronics supplier, understand not only *your* competition in the packaging industry but also the competition your counterparty faces in his part of the electronics industry. How do *his* competitors package their products? Always do your competitive homework beforehand, although some can be done in "real time" during the negotiation if you have Internet access.

KNOW YOUR ALTERNATIVES

The Importance of BATNA (Best Alternative to a Negotiated Agreement)

You're in the middle of the negotiation about your new room addition. Suddenly things take a turn, and you're not at all sure this contractor is on the same page as you are. Maybe he doesn't understand what you are looking for, the price is too high or the completion date is too far out. He seems unprepared. What do you do? How do you move the negotiation forward? What did you, or should you, have prepared in advance of the negotiation to deal with this possibility?

Getting what you want—and getting a negotiation back on track—often requires having alternatives—a Plan B and maybe a Plan C for what you will do if Plan A doesn't hold water. In this case, Plan B might be a different project design and spec; Plan C might be a different contractor.

Such alternatives, which obviously must be prepared for in advance, do a couple of things: first they set your expectations for what you can get; and second they give you alternative bargaining chips ("Well, you know, Contractor XYZ can do this by June for a thousand dollars less").

Having one or several alternative courses of action is key to negotiating successfully; indeed it will give you an advantage. You need to know what other counterparties are available to do the same thing, just as you want to know about all the stores that carry that super-high-definition TV you covet. Alternatives provide you with the confidence to reject offers and to walk away from the negotiation if you're not happy with the way it's going. Alternatives can give you negotiating power.

For example, imagine that there's only one car dealership in your town, and you need a car. You'll be disappointed if your negotiations with the car dealer don't go at all the way you had hoped. The dealer is well aware that his business is your only option, and thus he holds all the power, taking full advantage of the situation by offering no concessions. Under such circumstances, you'd want to find an alternative car to buy or visit the dealer in the next town—or not buy at all (doing nothing is a good alternative in many negotiations).

ESTABLISHING A PLAN B

Whatever you're negotiating, you should have at least one Plan B that's as beneficial as your original plan—else your effort to move the negotiation forward turns into a simple concession and you may not be content with the outcome if Plan A fails. Plan B should be carefully cultivated under the assumption that it's actually an A Plan. The same amount of research, prodding, and strategizing should occur so that you can spring right back into action if your original plan falls through. The more solid alternatives you have under your belt, the more poise you'll exhibit in front of the other party.

Using Alternatives to Your Advantage

Unquestionably the other party will bring a set of alternatives to the table. It pays to find out what alternatives the counterparty is considering. Discovering what other options your counterparty has lined up allows you to assess his confidence level and leverage in the negotiation. If he doesn't have any options, or the ones you perceive he does have are weak, then you have the upper hand. You may have the upper hand to drive for some concessions—but again, remember the importance of a win-win and the long-term relationship if you intend to negotiate with this counterparty again. Remember also that *you* may have no good alternatives next time around.

KNOW YOUR BATNA

In their renowned book *Getting to Yes* (1991, revised 2011), Roger Fisher and William Ury suggest going into a negotiation not just with a "bottom line"—the minimum agreement you're willing to accept—but also with an intermediate level of success in mind. That intermediate level of success becomes the standard by which you measure and compare the ultimate outcome.

Fisher and Ury refer to that intermediate standard as a Best Alternative to a Negotiated Agreement, or BATNA. Here's how it works. As you enter a negotiation, try to visualize the bottom line, as we've described it. You're about to negotiate for a raise, and the minimum you'll accept is a basic cost of living increase, say, 2 percent. That's your bottom line.

You'll most likely settle for that amount if you can't get anything better. Without a predetermined alternative, or intermediary level of acceptance, what happens? Many negotiators end up settling for this minimum acceptable bottom line because it's the only thing they know for sure as a set standard as they go through the preparation phase.

Instead, Fisher and Ury's idea is to set a BATNA—a best alternative—as a guideline as you enter the negotiation. It may be an explicit alternative, like interviewing and receiving an offer for another job before you enter the negotiation. Or it might be an established "not go below" point on the wage scale, often with some other perk or benefit involved (reimbursement for parking, a private office, or some such).

A BATNA is established during the preparation phase. You can establish more than one alternative if you have the time and bandwidth to craft multiple alternatives (one should emerge as "best"). If you have a clearly established BATNA, you're more likely to settle for *it*—not the minimum acceptable outcome. You have something better to measure your negotiation against, and in many cases it can become a bargaining chip, as in the case of the alternative job offer.

Fast Prep versus Full Prep

Many times—I'll speculate—most times, you won't have the time to do the full preparation that you think the negotiation might require. You won't have time to research alternatives, compare competitors, learn about your counterparties, etc. And this is true whether it's a complex negotiation or a discussion with your twelve-year-old daughter over bedtime. You won't have time to get the whole story.

Here is where the Pareto Principle—the 80–20 rule—enjoys no finer hour. The principle, simply put, is that you invest 20 percent of the prep time to get 80 percent of the story. In the office, you might do a brief price survey, competitive survey, and counterparty assessment. At home, you ask your twelve-year-old daughter a few "why" questions. Go wide—try to get at least *some* information about every topic and characteristic that might influence the negotiation. Then, if you have the time, circle back and add *more* competitors, *more* price points, *more* service extras, *more* knowledge about the counterparty. Develop a core presentation, then add to it. Such a well-rounded, iterative, add-as-you-can approach will make you seem more prepared, and you probably will be. As in many things in business and life—work *smart*, not just hard.

THE MEETING ITSELF

How to Prepare for the Day of the Show

Business negotiation meetings used to all occur in a physical location like a conference room or meeting room, somewhere in an office or hotel, or some other defined venue. Today, business negotiations, and most personal negotiations, can happen almost anywhere, anytime—often over email or by phone. Most of the more important negotiations are planned, but many can occur spontaneously, on the go, and in segments (a couple of phone calls and a meeting, for instance). However and wherever the negotiation is to occur is part of your preparation process.

With planned negotiations, there is an opportunity for some strategy and control of the meeting, including the place, time, and agenda. With unplanned or spontaneous negotiations, you can still control the meeting to a degree (if you want to) by simply stating that you can't negotiate now—why not do it later at a time and place of mutual agreement?

MANAGING THE AGENDA

Preparing an agenda for the meeting is one way to control the pace and timing of the meeting, and doing so will help you stay focused and (hopefully!) keep everyone on track as well. The agenda itself is usually negotiable with the counterparty; in fact, this can be a crucial entry point to the negotiation. The agenda should allow for discovery, presentation of alternatives, and making the deal. Other actions, such as further research constructive to the deal, may need to be accommodated.

The agenda sequence, presenters, topics, desired outcomes, time allotted, and "free" time and even breaks and lunches are all important elements of the agenda. The agenda should steer the conversation toward the goals you want to achieve. This can be accomplished by managing time allotments for factual presentations, discussions, and establishing desired outcomes. By controlling the agenda you control the pace of the process, and the process can proceed in synch with your objectives. It also helps to be the discussion moderator or leader. In such a role you can adjust the meeting content and format, often in real time, to achieve what you want to achieve.

The Agenda Is More Than a Schedule!

Think there's no use for an agenda in a quick negotiation? Think again! It helps to lay out a quick-and-dirty agenda even for a simple phone call or email discussion. This gets the other party to agree on what the objective is, how much time will be spent on each topic, and what the desired outcome is, even if the negotiation is just for a few minutes. An agenda helps to keep things on track, and it helps you avoid leaving important items out. It also gives you some control over the meeting and hence, the negotiation. Always think in terms of setting—and controlling—the agenda.

KNOW THE VENUE

Many complex negotiations involve meeting rooms, presentations, and discussions. As you might guess, any breakdown or awkwardness in your delivery of your presentations, and any ambiguity in the compilations of the results in the negotiation, can be detrimental.

Worse, these problems can reflect badly on you and weaken your reputation as a negotiator—even temporarily.

You should prepare in advance to make sure you understand how all the audio-visual equipment works and decide in advance how meeting notes and decisions will be captured. Will you have a note taker? Electronic note pad and printer? Large white paper pad on an easel? Decide up front—don't scramble when your counterparty arrives.

Know where the bathrooms are, know the Wi-Fi passwords, set up any computer or projection equipment in advance if you can; have the show ready to go.

You get extra credit for helping your counterparties get set up, too. You'll get credit for being a team player and for coming out ahead in your negotiation on its merits—not because they couldn't get their laptop to synch with your projector. Knowing the venue for yourself and helping your counterparties get engaged will help both today's negotiation and your reputation for the long term.

BEING PREPARED FOR TAKE ONE

A Filmographic Productions Case Study

You're the president, CEO, and CVO (Chief Video Officer) of Filmographic Productions, a small firm (really, just you most of the time) engaged in commercial video production mainly in your local market. You have some helpers and associates you contract with on an as-needed basis, and your brother-in-law, a stay-at-home dad, helps you from time to time with administrative work to arrange for actors and venues and to edit videos. You have a range of other suppliers and services, including a talent agency and a helicopter service at your disposal for aerial photos, among others.

You are trying to secure a deal with a big client: Dewey and Cheatum Associates, a local financial services firm. They would like you to produce short commercials and videos for their website extolling the virtues of their services. You want to get a juicy regular gig shooting new commercials every month. If you get an "exclusive" for this job, it would mean an extra $15,000 to $20,000 in monthly revenues, which would go a long way toward making your year.

But you must negotiate successfully.

So, as we've learned in this chapter, that means among other things you must:

1. Set good goals.
2. Know and understand your client.
3. Evaluate alternatives and concessions so as to secure at least part of the business for yourself with terms sufficient to sustain your business.
4. Be prepared for the day of the negotiation.

Following is a brief summary of the thought process you might go through. If you were doing this for real, these might be more completely thought out and documented, something you might do yourself or with a partner or sounding board over a nice dinner or refreshments.

GOAL SETTING

Main goal: Get all the business; become Dewey's exclusive video producer for your local market.

Secondary goals: Get a substantial portion of the business, say, the monthly commercials only. Build a relationship so they will call you to produce one-time or ad hoc, irregular pieces of business You also want them to come to you with new ideas for producing video shorts for their business.

Stretch goal: Get their business in other cities and markets. Beyond that, you might hope they recommend your services to *their* customers and clients when it makes sense.

PLANNING CONCESSIONS AND ALTERNATIVES

Videographers have myriads of negotiation concessions at their disposal. They can offer free samples, they can give rights to the videos or not, they can arrange for a full service, including venue selection and actor training—or not. Production and delivery time is another important factor. A best alternative, or BATNA, might be to use their personnel in videos in their banks instead of hiring professional actors. It could mean non-high-definition video. It could even mean partnering with a firm they're already using, if that firm brings special abilities to the table you don't have and vice versa. Think big here—you need to be ready to put together a package deal.

As the chief negotiator (as well as chief of everything else), you need to know how much time, effort, and cost is involved in each alternative on your list. Do the research beforehand. Prepare a list of options and know what each one costs, and be ready to respond immediately when you get a question or hear a competitive offer from the Dewey negotiator. It helps to have such a menu of services right on your laptop or some other device. It also helps—and this can be done online—to be able to review some samples of services delivered to other clients. "For ABC and Associates, I did X, Y, and Z for $abcd . . ." Fast, friendly, and effective negotiating means having all of these figures at your fingertips.

KNOW YOUR CLIENT

Research your client from top to bottom—corporate structure, previous advertising and website efforts, and individuals involved (through Google, LinkedIn, Facebook, and other sources). Observe their commercials and videos on their website for your city and other cities they might do business in; get an idea of what they like. Ask questions to learn more about the structure of their organization. How are decisions made? Do the local managers decide on photo services, or is there a corporate marketing team that makes the call? Once you get the job, who would work with you? You'll have a different relationship if you're working with someone in graphic arts versus a marketing department, or with an operations manager or advertising director or webmaster. Learn all that you can about their internal rules for the purchase of marketing services.

PREPARE FOR THE MEETING

Know the venue. Will you have Internet access during the negotiation, so that you can retrieve and show video image samples or previous video service prices? Will you be able to effectively show your samples? Will there be a projector that you can hook into your laptop? Can you check to make sure the laptop-projector connection works correctly before the negotiation?

These questions and conceptual frameworks are designed only to get you started. As you might imagine, the "prepare" stage can go quite deep, and it may require a lot of time. But remember—a prepared negotiator has a huge advantage over an unprepared negotiator.

With the right preparation, there will be many "takes" to this story.

Chapter 4

Negotiating Styles and Personalities— Yours and Theirs

In Chapter 3 I stressed the idea of broad preparation for any negotiation, covering everything from goals, musts, and wants to the details of the product, price, and competitive landscape, all the way to knowing your counterparty and the negotiating venue. This broad view tells you what to prepare; as you approach the negotiation, you'll want to dive into the detail of these areas as time and access to information permit.

As you try to "see the outcome," you should recognize that one of the key variables is the negotiating style of the counterparty— particularly the main spokesperson of the counterparty. The interpersonal dynamic between you and the members of your team—and the leader and the members of the counterparty team—can have a lot to do with the final outcome.

This chapter is about "seeing" the negotiation style you'll have to deal with (and understanding your own, don't forget), and then getting a handle on how your styles mesh and how to counteract the differences in style. Put simply, oil and water at the negotiating table will not bring the best win-win agreement.

In this chapter I will examine the ins and outs of seven distinct negotiating styles, give some additional insight into negotiating personalities—the building blocks of negotiating styles—and then finish with a summary of how to deal with difficult styles and personalities.

WHY IS STYLE IMPORTANT?

Negotiators Are People, and People Are Different

As you start to internalize the basics of negotiating (why negotiate, what to negotiate for, how to give and take, and how to prepare) you should also keep in mind other important pieces of the puzzle. One of these is *people*. No matter what the negotiation is about, at the end of the day, you're negotiating with people. Negotiators come from all walks of life—all personalities, all experiences, and all styles. They can be professional negotiators or negotiating professionals (remember the difference?). They can be people just like you, but many times they're not like you at all!

Part of the preparation process involves understanding and recognizing the different negotiating styles, personality styles, and personas you'll find in the negotiating world. Not only will you encounter these styles, but you'll most likely adopt one or more of them yourself, depending on the situation, your objectives, and your own personality. In today's fast-negotiation world, you may have to recognize these styles very quickly and do so through relatively impersonal means, i.e. not by face-to-face communication.

Below I will identify seven common negotiating "styles" you'll often find across the negotiating table, one of which likely describes you as well! If someone is an "intimidator," can you recognize that through initial contacts? The quicker you can, the better.

THE INTIMIDATOR

Intimidators prey on emotions. They employ tactics that may not seem fair to you, because they try to keep you off balance and prevent you from thinking clearly. They want you to feel as if the negotiation is personal—and if something goes wrong it's your fault. They put you on the defensive and try to separate you from your rational self. They hope your bruised ego will prevent you from looking objectively at the negotiation as it unfolds.

Is this psychological warfare? You bet! Intimidators take advantage of your human side, focusing less on the business aspect of what you're trying to accomplish and more on the personal side. They hope you'll do anything—give anything—to seek peace and find balance in the negotiation, even if it means your side has to cede ground. They hope you never regain equilibrium; that you give in to their demands just so you can be done with this phase of the deal.

Remember: a deal done under stress and duress is likely to be a bad deal.

RECOGNIZABLE CHARACTERISTICS

If your counterparty is shouting or pounding a fist or slapping papers down on the table, you're seeing an intimidator in action. These people are loud, talk fast, make hurried movements, and often resort to profanity to make a point. They interrupt constantly. Again, they're trying to get you to focus on the antics, to prevent you from thinking clearly, to distract you and cause you to lose your train of thought, especially when they don't like what they're hearing or they're not getting their way. They want you to jump from rational negotiator mode to "people pleaser" mode, to jump from getting what you want to placating *their* needs. Don't go there!

Intimidators will make demands, not suggestions or requests. Rather than accepting that you're proposing a workable solution benefiting both of you, they'll tell you that they're insulted by an offer of anything less than exactly what they demanded in the first place. They may start yelling again and even throw out a few expletives for extra drama.

Intimidators push you around and try to frighten or annoy you with threats. They might threaten to call off the entire negotiation or to bring in someone from upper management or to withdraw their business altogether. Quite often these behaviors are bluffs; you should handle them accordingly.

Be aware that not all intimidators are loud and blustery. Some may take the quiet approach, shrewdly manipulating you with a barely recognizable yet penetrating insolence. Their ploy may even be delivered more through body language than verbal antagonism. Condescending by nature, they know how to crawl under your skin with just a look, hand gesture, or blink of an eye. They may not intimidate you with brazen scare tactics but may instead act as if they're far above you in every way.

Whatever the approach, an intimidator may just patronize your business sense. But when an intimidator also patronizes your person—look out!

Counteracting the Intimidator

The best way to defend against intimidators is to avoid stooping to their level. Stay calm, focused, and in control. When the intimidator starts raising his voice, keep yours at an even tone. Displaying no emotion whatsoever and going on about your business shows them that you won't take the bait. You're a professional, and your objective is to reach an agreement, not to get into a fight.

Dealing with the Intimidator in Presidential Politics

In late 2016, the "going about your business" tactic was clearly on display in the first presidential debate of the fall 2016 campaign. Donald Trump ranted, showed emotion, and even exhibited annoying and sometimes aggressive body language and stage positioning to his counterparty, Hillary Clinton. But she didn't flinch, and she simply went on about her business. That got under his skin, and he showed even more of that behavior—which left a negative impression on the audience and caused him, as much as anything else, to "lose" that first debate.

As we found out from the election results, countermanding the intimidator may not always win in the end. Nonetheless, rising above the bluster can help you out a lot along the way.

Never shout or use abusive language. That only escalates the conflict and takes you away from the issue at hand. Instead, stay calm, focused, and in control. Avoid emotional involvement and work to get the focus back on the issues at hand. Ask open-ended questions to avoid being brushed off with simple yes-and-no answers. Your goal is to force your counterparty to talk about the issues, the real reasons you're both there. In so doing the intimidator might cool down and realize you aren't playing his game.

If he tries to intimidate you by threatening to pull out of the negotiation altogether, try to feel out how serious this threat is. Offer a few noncritical concessions—or ask point blank what he plans to do if he pulls out. The goal is to call his bluff. If he leaves the table as an intimidation tactic, remember that he'll probably be back if your negotiating position is solid to begin with—and he'll be weaker as a result of the called bluff. It's a gamble on your part but one probably worth taking to neutralize the intimidation.

As in the case of most negotiations gone sour or uncomfortable, it helps to take a time-out to regroup and cool the emotions. You'll cool your own, and you're likely to diminish the thunder of your opponent, particularly if it was a ploy in the first place. You might even ask him point blank, over a refreshment, "Why are you being so angry and difficult to talk to? We could get this done much quicker and more effectively if we simply hold ourselves as equals and have a productive conversation." As you might surmise, this tactic works in both business and personal negotiations.

THE FLATTERER

Positive, Complimentary—and Insincere

Like the intimidator, the flatterer focuses more on your emotions than on facts and logic. The difference: the flatterer gets personal by loading the negotiation with positive but insincere remarks. The idea, once again, is to get an emotional response, deflect you from the facts, and throw you off balance.

The flatterer operates under the assumption (mostly correct) that everyone loves to receive compliments, so she lays it on to boost your ego. You may hear glowingly positive comments about your business style, your product, your team, your company, or even your personal appearance. When the car salesperson tells you how good you look driving in a particular car, take the compliment with a grain of salt.

The point of this ego stroking is to appeal to your emotional side, to give you a false sense of reality, even a false sense of security. For example, the flatterer may try to make you believe that you have the upper hand—that you're "winning" the negotiation—so why not "give us a break" and offer a few minor concessions?

RECOGNIZABLE CHARACTERISTICS

Since the flatterer attempts to render the negotiation more personal than professional, you might see a lot of smiles and compliments right off the bat. Throughout the negotiation, your counterparty might say something like, "I know I can't pull one over on you, Amanda, that's why I'm giving it to you straight right now." The hope is that you'll be so flattered at the recognition of your expert, seasoned negotiating skills that you'll bask in the glory, become complacent, and ultimately lose your edge in the negotiation.

Keep an Eye on the Faces

Since extreme flattery is a form of dishonesty, its presence can be a good indicator as to whether the other party plans to fulfill her side of the bargain. Try to recognize speech patterns and facial expressions when the flattering statement is made—and compare those patterns to what you see when the counterparty agrees with one of your requests.

Never underestimate the ability of body language, facial expressions, and speech to tell you what's really going on.

When the other party turns you into the main subject of the discussion, it becomes a challenge to stay focused on the details of the issues you're talking about. It's easy to get sucked into all that flattery, not to mention the pleasant, nonconfrontational language. We all like to hear nice things about ourselves. But you must focus on your purpose for the negotiation, which is to achieve business (or personal) goals in a win-win approach—not to have your ego stroked.

Counteracting the Flatterer

The first and most obvious step is to recognize flattery and see it for what it is. The flatterer, like the intimidator, is an expert at tapping into your emotions. Such an approach is not only a style but a habit. Your approach should be the same as with the intimidator: Redirect the focus back to the issues at hand. Stop and redirect the conversation, even start taking notes, as it shows the counterparty you mean business. Stay calm, ignore the flattery, and don't let it frustrate you. Redirect by asking open-ended questions that force your counterparty to talk about the details of the negotiation.

Another defensive tactic is to change your tone of voice to one of total indifference. Don't use inflections or interject any personality into your speech. If you project a steely, emotionless image to the other party and refuse to react to the sweet talk, she will eventually realize that you're not succumbing to her tactics.

Another tactic is to involve a third party, either one present at the negotiation or brought in for the task. Getting a manager or technical expert involved can help—it takes the focus off you and once again redirects the negotiation to the facts and to the results. When you get flattered by a car salesperson, it's time to bring in your spouse or grown child to diffuse the flattery. In business, bringing in another party, especially a manager or other authority, will help.

Aside from letting the flattery get you off track, the worst thing you can do is return the flattery. Don't go there. If you do, she's roped you into a mutual admiration compact and opened the door for more flattery and even less serious negotiating. Don't go there.

THE SEDUCER

Magic Through Charm?

You've most definitely experienced this one before—if not in business life, certainly in your personal life. The seducer works his magic through charm. He paints a perfect picture for you and describes everything exactly as you want to hear it. But the devil is in the details—when you start to investigate, the illusion just as magically disappears. The ideal image you had in mind, one that you might have just made a concession for, disappears as you uncover more details.

You're about to get a new credit card to get that special deal and 10 percent off on that home theater system? Sounds like a good idea and a nice concession on the part of the electronics retailer. By all appearances, it's a win-win deal. Only after they ring you up at the register do you find out that the rebate comes after the fact as store credit coupons that you must use to buy something else rather than applying it toward the home theater purchase. The salesperson/negotiator made the discount a central part of the deal, only to pull the rug out from under you. You were seduced.

RECOGNIZABLE CHARACTERISTICS

The seducer is crafty and sometimes unethical, and he will make attractive offers and concessions to you throughout the negotiating process. Once he has you hooked, he'll reel you in by telling you what you want to hear—often in half-truths. "You'll get 10 percent off"—but it isn't a discount, it's a credit toward your next purchase. As soon as you make the commitment, he points to the fine print, and the deal he really offered begins to emerge.

The seducer may blame "the system" behind him. You'll hear excuses like, "The paperwork is still being finalized," "My manager hasn't authorized it yet," or "I'm waiting to hear from my attorney." The deal may be sped up—or slowed down—to meet his objective. He might speed it up to get you out of the store before you notice; or he might slow it down by distracting you with some other detail, a phone call or contingency so once again, you don't notice the change in the promise. When the counterparty seems to be deliberately speeding up or slowing down, look out.

Counteracting the Seducer

Protecting yourself from the seducer is simple: Don't deal. Make the seducing point seem unimportant or irrelevant: "I was planning to pay cash anyway." If it's too late and the agreement has been made, revisit the negotiation and get a higher authority involved—an attorney or a manager or some such person. Even the threat to do that can neutralize the counterparty. He may retract the seducing element(s) on his own. If you've recognized the signs early on, simply leave the negotiation and seek other alternatives.

Research can be your best friend here. The more you find out about the party you'll be dealing with in negotiations, the better your chances of identifying a seducer early and staying out of the way. If you're shopping for electronics, for instance, a review of the seller's website or a flip through their weekly ad circular can clue you in to the types of deals you may hear about on the sales floor.

If you decide to continue negotiating with the seducer, be sure to be informed of every detail of the agreements made. Ask lots of questions. Know what you're getting and how you're getting it. Facts neutralize the seducer, as they do many other types of negotiators who appeal to your emotions. Take notes where appropriate. It lets the seducer know you're paying attention to every word.

Finally, be skeptical. A little healthy skepticism never hurts in any negotiation.

THE COMPLAINER

Working the Guilt Angle

Although the complainer is not as deceitful and unfair as other negotiating personalities covered thus far, she can still undermine the
negotiation. The complainer is typically an insecure negotiator—or
a master at the ploy—who really wants to be heard and understood.
Once she's gotten her say, this counterparty becomes more reasonable and more pleasant to work with.

RECOGNIZABLE CHARACTERISTICS

Complainers succeed when they make you feel bad about what
you're asking for or what you need or want out of a negotiation. They
induce guilt, motivating you to moderate your requests in order to
keep them happy.

Complainers can sometimes come across as positional negotiators, not win-win negotiators (see Chapter 2). This is because they
don't appear to look past their own needs. They may appear not to
be willing to budge from their position, but really they're looking
for you to come up with the deal that makes them not complain
anymore.

You may hear statements like, "How can you expect me to give
you a free warranty when you're already asking me for a discount?"
or "You have no idea how expensive it is for production to make the
kinds of changes you're asking for," or "I'll get fired if I offer you *that*
deal." If you listen closely, there's a cry for help couched in those
sentences.

When complainers begin statements with "How can you" and "You have no idea," they really want you to back down a little and help them out. They can take a perceived weakness—if the ploy works—and turn it into a strength, thereby giving up less than they otherwise might have.

Counteracting the Complainer

You'll need a good ear and an empathetic heart to guard against the complainer. If you handle the situation with the right amount of patience and understanding, you'll get through the fluff and the apparent dug-in position. You can then help her realize that a win-win may well be in sight, which can in turn allay the fears and complaints. She wants your understanding, and perhaps you can give her some without giving away the store.

Don't Just Listen—Listen Actively!

No matter the negotiation, and no matter the style of the negotiators, your job doesn't end at simply being there, hearing, or even passively listening. You must listen *actively*. Paraphrase a few of the counterparty's key points to show empathy and a correct understanding of their situation. If you're conducting the conversation by email, repeat portions of the email when you reply to show you've read and understood the entire message.

Active listening is particularly effective with the complainer, but it works well in all walks of negotiating life. If you listen actively to them, they'll be more likely to listen actively to you. You'll find that win-win much more easily.

As soon as complainers start voicing concerns, hear them out. Hear every word they say, and encourage them to say more. Nod, make eye contact, and use hand gestures to let them know you're really listening. Listen actively, saying, "I see" or "That's understandable" as verbal acknowledgement. Once it's all let out, the burden is lifted and the counterparty will relax. Most likely she'll play well into your needs so as to get her complaints and negatives resolved.

Once you've finished listening to the complainer's viewpoint, ask more questions to slowly get back to the details of the negotiation. You might even offer a concession, a small one you saved for later, or one that you can afford to be flexible with. Show complainers that you see their point and will make an effort to make the negotiation successful for both them and you—a win-win.

THE ARGUER

For the Love of Conflict

No doubt you have certainly experienced this negotiator style in your personal life if not your business life. The arguer is a counterparty who seems to love the conflict, thriving on disagreement—and where there isn't a conflict or disagreement, he creates one just because that's where his comfort zone lies! What you'll see is a constant argument with the main points of a discussion—and/or more subtly, a steady and unrelenting nitpick of the smaller ones. Some arguers may start out calm and accommodating and then switch to an argumentative mode midstream in the negotiation.

RECOGNIZABLE CHARACTERISTICS

The arguer can be easily spotted by his steady and unprompted debates of your issues and requests. True, a negotiation can be a back-and-forth debate to get to an alternative everyone can agree on. But it turns into an argument when it gets loud and/or nitpicky and when one side or the other presses for the win. Arguers debate and nitpick more than necessary; it will seem as if they have trouble separating what's important from what isn't. They lay a lot of objections on unimportant stuff at your feet.

Counteracting the Arguer

The arguer may pounce on your every move toward progress, hoping to stall the negotiation and buy more time for his case, or to prove his ability to win something. Use the agenda created before the meeting to remind him that you're on a schedule and would like to stick to it to cover everything. Ignore aimless arguments by reacting to only the important ones.

When arguments dominate, ask the counterparty to explain the main concern of the argument. Focus on resolving that issue first, but be aware of meaningless arguments that might pop up along the way. It's easy to get so caught up trying to win smaller, insignificant disputes that the real issue at hand is often lost along the way. Some arguers argue as a means of distraction, hoping you'll inadvertently give something away; others behave this way out of a need to score as many victories as possible, large or small. Just keep asking yourself: Do I want to be right, or do I want to win? Often you can do both. But in many situations, being right at the expense of winning ultimately means winning the battle but losing the war.

As with other strong styles of negotiation, stick to your facts, ignore appeals to your emotions, and call time-outs where you think it might help. If it really gets bad, advise the counterparty that "things aren't working" and that you may be forced to leave the negotiation.

Above all, avoid becoming an arguer yourself; that will only feed the fire.

THE BSer

Stretching—or Ignoring—the Truth

Lies, lies, lies. Little white lies. Half-truths. Stretched truths. Exaggerations. Broken promises. All held to be harmless because—well—this is business, right?

It's interesting how the process of selling something (or marketing something or advertising something) seemingly empowers us all (most of us anyway) to embellish the truth—even just a little bit. We want to make our product, our service, our company sound better than the competition. We give ourselves the latitude to claim, "We're the best" even though there is no hard evidence to that effect.

A BSer in a negotiation stretches the truth (or in the worst cases, ignores it altogether) to get what she wants. You may see this through your personal "lie detector." You may notice shifty eyes, broken voice (or extra firm voice) and feel that something just isn't right. What she says seems to be more what you want to hear than the truth; it just doesn't pass the smell test.

RECOGNIZABLE CHARACTERISTICS

Honed from experience, both in business and our personal lives, we all have our own personal BS detectors. When something seems too good to be true, it usually is. Statements unsupported by facts or supported more by pomp and ebullience than facts are dead giveaways. Large quantities of superlatives can also tip you off—most, best, least, cheapest. Loss of eye contact, a change in a speech pattern, and general nervousness can all indicate a lie or exaggeration.

It's true that some exaggeration and hyperbole comes with the business territory, particularly with gray areas that are difficult to support with facts. Our minds tend to wrap around our own products as best, and when we go into selling or evangelizing mode ourselves, it's natural to want others on our bandwagon. "Ours is the most beautiful on the road" isn't a lie, it's a matter of judgment—but if you hear too many such statements, look out.

Counteracting the BSer

The best way to counteract the BSer is to call her out by asking her to support her statements. Don't be bashful about this—simply state that getting the facts is important for you to have proper confidence in the negotiation. If you call out the facts repeatedly, you'll make it clear that you're onto her style and ploy—particularly if you find she's repeatedly gotten the facts wrong.

The BSer tries to take control of the meeting and get the upper hand by fabricating ideas for you to swallow. If you swallow too many untruths and exaggerations, you open the door to more and more of them. It happens all the time in the business and personal world. Keep in mind, BS only works when you believe it. Simple advice: don't. Let your counterparty know early on that you're onto any lies, you will seek the truth even if it's uncomfortable, and that if she continues to bend the truth, you'll depart from the negotiation. You don't have time for this.

Most of all, don't go into BS mode yourself. Fighting fire with fire only makes the fire bigger. Everyone gets burned eventually. Honesty is the best policy—always.

THE LOGICAL THINKER

Analysis Paralysis

Logical thinkers, naturally, can be quite reasonable to work with. However, in some cases they tend to overanalyze issues and linger on them too long. They often nitpick and bring up valid points that you might acknowledge but not necessarily agree with. If you don't agree, they probe your reasons why. If you do agree, that encourages them to probe some more.

The main problem with logical thinkers is that through this constant questioning of details they create a lot of what should be "parking lot" discussions that sidetrack the negotiation. (I call these "parking lot" discussions because they're the kind that should happen in the parking lot when you're all done with the main discussion and are getting ready to get in your car and leave.) The challenge is to keep focus and avoid going off into the weeds to overanalyze minor issues.

That said, all but the most detail-adverse negotiators typically like to work with logical thinkers. They are insightful and don't play emotional mind games to try to get you off course. They may derail you through their analysis and requests for detail, but this is a genuine part of their nature, not a negotiating tactic. If you satisfy their needs for detail, the win-win comes easier.

RECOGNIZABLE CHARACTERISTICS

The logical thinker deals in facts and figures. Most are naturally skeptical, and most ask a lot of questions. They emphasize detail.

Their questions may seem frivolous or beside the point to you, but they aren't to the logical thinking counterparty. The logical thinker is trying to draw conclusions, test the validity of your statements and claims, weed out inaccuracies, and evaluate information.

Occasionally you may run into a counterparty who isn't a logical thinker but who uses intense questioning and analysis to get you off balance or to "filibuster" a deal he doesn't want. You can usually recognize this ploy by the frivolity of the questions and whether he appears to be listening or responding to your answers.

Counteracting the Logical Thinker

The best way to deal with the logical thinker is to make every statement clear and back each up by sound research. Don't use jargon or statistics and facts you can't support. Be mindful that every person who asks a question isn't employing the logical thinker style of negotiating—you'll figure it out by the persistence of questions, the level of detail, and how the questioner responds to the answers. If he appears to be analyzing the facts and your answers to his questions, he fits the logical thinker mold.

Basically you want to try to play his game. Satisfy his needs for information. Be a logical thinker yourself—ask a lot of questions yourself and demand facts to back up assertions. The logical thinker will respond well to this. But at the same time, it's a good idea to assume leadership of the meeting, politely keep it on track and out of the weeds, and keep the agenda and the ultimate win-win deal front and center. Don't hesitate to take breaks when things go off track. You can discuss some of those nagging details during your break, but come back ready to discuss the substantive topics on your agenda.

NEGOTIATING PERSONALITIES

Deep Down Behind a Negotiating Style

So far in this chapter, we've discussed negotiating *styles*—which, not surprisingly, are a function of an individual's personality. In this section we'll take apart those styles to discover the specific building blocks of a negotiator's personality—the core elements of personality that are a part of someone's negotiating style.

Negotiating styles are chosen and developed by the individuals who deploy them, while negotiating personalities are innate; they are a natural and typically unchangeable part of someone's being. Just as you can recognize a negotiating style and deal with it over the table, you can also learn to recognize personalities. This section will help you do that. Armed with this knowledge, you can create a checklist of ways to deal with the different personalities. This section will also help you better understand your own negotiating personality. Finally, assessing your counterparty's negotiating personality during the preparation phase, if possible, will create a more effective negotiation.

I will cover six negotiating personalities: Aggressive/Dominating, Passive/Submissive, Logical/Analytical, Friendly/Collaborative, Evasive/Uncooperative, and Expressive/Communicative. As you might surmise, it is possible for a negotiator to exhibit more than one of these personalities.

AGGRESSIVE/DOMINATING

You've no doubt dealt with an aggressive personality. This personality is motivated by power and influence, and manifests itself in the following familiar traits:

- Demanding
- Pushy
- Bossy
- Self-centered
- Controlling
- Defensive
- Competitive
- Persistent
- Power junkie (enjoys power and respects people in power)
- Forceful
- Challenging
- Disdainful of weakness
- Rude
- Vengeful
- Easily angered
- Dominant
- Intimidating
- Ambitious
- Successful
- Impatient
- Shrewd
- Fast learning

How They Operate

Individuals with aggressive/dominating "driver" personalities tend to talk fast and act fast. They don't want to spend any more time with you than necessary. They're usually busy; they thrive in a fast-paced work environment. Preparing to negotiate with them means that you need to have all the facts in order beforehand, and be ready for a speedy discussion. Their patience is in short supply; they will rush you along every chance they get. For an aggressive/dominating individual, a negotiation becomes all about control pretty quickly.

As negotiators, aggressive personality types want to win as much as they can and give as little as possible. Victory is their main goal, and they're used to getting their own way. They may adopt a positional negotiating style, caring little for how you fare in the deal. When they don't get their way, they can become agitated and even more difficult to deal with.

Playing Defense

"Fight fire with fire" may be one defensive tactic. Or you can try to slow them down by being cool, calm, and matter-of-fact. Adhering to a well-structured agenda can also help. Turning the floor over to someone else in the room or on a call can help, too. Be cool, play steady, avoid emotional responses, and stick to the facts and the win-win mantra.

PASSIVE/SUBMISSIVE

This personality is the exact opposite of the aggressive/dominating personality. Passive/submissive negotiators tend to exhibit the following characteristics:

- Nice, friendly
- Considerate
- Insecure
- Uncomfortable with conflict
- Fear not being liked
- Sensitive
- Shy

- Introverted
- Good listener
- Loner
- Calm
- Reserved
- Avoid being the center of attention
- Prefer to work alone or with few people rather than in groups
- Obedient
- Quiet

How They Operate

Passive/submissive negotiators are typically more focused on pleasing other people than on the mechanics of the negotiation itself. They are often taken advantage of; but watch out. It's easy to misinterpret these attributes—an aggressive wolf can reside in sheep's clothing! Truly submissive negotiators want others to like them. They'll do whatever they can to make the other party happy, even if it means giving extra concessions or letting the other party renege on one of theirs. They are well suited to win-win negotiations, but they may be inclined to give up too much too early.

Submissive personalities seldom take control of the negotiation. They don't like the limelight, and they're more comfortable following than leading. They don't want to cause chaos or disturb the peace, so they rarely speak out of turn or voice their thoughts and opinions.

Watch Out for Passive-Aggressives

As a variant of submissive behavior, you might be dealing with passive-aggressive behavior, where calm, polite, or even reticent behavior masks more aggressive notions under the surface. Such behavior, perhaps initially

assessed as pushover behavior, may come back to bite you later in the negotiation or after the negotiation. It can be hard to spot.

One tactic for discovering passive-aggressive behavior is to lay out a small task, a request, or an open issue within the negotiation. Let the counterparty take the item to research or decide on during the meeting and report back to you before the end. She typically will accept the item politely or with little response. When she gets back to you, assess the aggressiveness of her response. If she doesn't accomplish your request at all, or does something different than what you asked, she probably falls into the passive-aggressive camp.

Playing Defense

No defense is required, save for the passive-aggressive variant noted in the sidebar. When you see passive-aggressive behavior, switch into aggressive defense mode—stick to agendas, facts, and the common purpose of the negotiation. Don't give in to this behavior.

You may have to work to draw out the true needs or agenda of a passive/submissive negotiator. Work hard to preserve the relationship so that you may get invited back for subsequent negotiations. Although you may be tempted to take advantage of a passive/submissive counterparty, resist doing so—a win-win preserves the relationship and future negotiating opportunities.

LOGICAL/ANALYTICAL

Analytical personalities tend to exhibit the following traits:

- Probing
- Apprehensive

- Mistrusting
- Fact-checker
- Thoughtful
- Organized
- Prepared
- Thinker
- Always early or on time
- Even-keeled
- Thrive on information
- Thorough with details
- Take time with decisions
- Insensitive
- Logical
- Fair
- Firm
- Critical

Logical/analytical negotiators must have all the facts, details, and information about the negotiation. They favor thorough preparation and have no desire to rush ahead.

How They Operate

Analyzers like to solve problems and seek deeper understanding of what they already know. They are achievers and have a strong sense of accomplishment—that is more important to them than power in the negotiation. In fact, they seek to achieve power through knowledge and achievement, not through exhibitions of personality or hierarchy and credentials.

Expect logical/analytical personalities to walk into the meeting room armed with data and facts. During the discussion you may feel

like you're being closely scrutinized, as if you're under a microscope. The counterparty seeks errors and inconsistencies in your presentation. This may come across as overcritical, but logical analyzers typically seek comfort in covering all bases before making a decision. You should prepare by knowing the facts and by being ready to research them on the fly if necessary.

Playing Defense

It's simple—be prepared. When possible, have documentation to back up your materials. Prepared graphs, charts, slides, and reports can all help. Don't bluff, stretch the truth, skew the facts, or tell half-truths—you're likely to be discovered. Prepare to be on trial. Try to help your counterparty get his facts together, draw conclusions, and make decisions (he may need help with the latter!).

A Little Pressure Can Go a Long Way

Logical/analytical negotiators often take a long time to make decisions. They tend to be a little insecure with the facts they have; they feel as if there's one more element to be explored. Try to reassure them, and feather in a little push or two along the way to help them get through their analysis and work toward the close. Left to their own devices, they might never do that.

FRIENDLY/COLLABORATIVE

The one most of us like best—the friendly and collaborative negotiator—is easy to recognize:

- Fair
- Courteous
- Empathetic
- Considerate
- Appreciative
- Understanding
- Honest
- Tactful
- Warm
- Friendly
- Successful
- Open-minded
- Resourceful
- Sincere
- Patient
- General concern for others
- Ability to employ creative thinking techniques
- Flexible
- Sensitive
- Tolerant
- Character and integrity

Such friendly/collaborator negotiators possess the principles needed to reach win-win solutions. They understand that a negotiation is not a battle. Rather it's an opportunity to attain mutual success with the least amount of resistance and negativity.

How They Operate
Collaborators are concerned with working toward results quickly and with everyone's agreement. They want to build trust and develop

solid relationships for the future. They try to learn as much as possible about their counterparties and their objectives so that the desired outcome can be achieved.

You're in luck when negotiating with a collaborator. You'll recognize the warm smile and friendly bearing. She listens and listens well. But don't be fooled—these negotiators possess a keen business sense and, at day's end, place the importance of task above you and above the relationship. They are true professionals.

Another Wolf?

Earlier I described the passive-aggressive personality. A quiet and polite demeanor might be mistaken for submissive behavior. Sometimes, though, this is a wolf in sheep's clothing, as this quiet personality will agitate to undermine the negotiation or ignore your requests and agreements sometime down the road.

A similar wolf can wear the disguise of an outwardly friendly and cohesive personality. This wolf waits until you become comfortable—*too* comfortable—and then pounces. If you have been to a car dealer, chances are you have seen this behavior in action. They show you around, let you test drive the car, answer all your questions; they're your best friend. Then suddenly they open their drawer and grab a sales contract form and start talking monthly payments—so much for your comfort! This sort of behavior is collaborative to a point. And at the point where you get sucked in, the negotiating fireworks begin. Don't be oversold on a counterparty's apparent friendly and collaborative nature.

Playing Defense

No defense is really necessary—except to make sure the behavior is genuine, not forced. To test this, you might throw an unreasonable request her way to see how she deals with it. If things suddenly become confrontational, then "collaborator" probably isn't her true personality. Be honest in your dealings with a genuinely friendly/collaborative negotiator so that your counterparty sees you as being collaborative, too.

EVASIVE/UNCOOPERATIVE

Some negotiators will seem reluctant to negotiate or even to be there at all. These negotiators tend to exhibit the following characteristics:

- Insecure
- Fearful
- Careful
- Play it safe
- Don't like confrontation
- Introverted
- Timid
- Calm
- Reserved
- Procrastinator
- Nonresponsive
- Cold
- Pessimistic
- Easily embarrassed
- Indifferent

Evasive/uncooperative negotiators deal with issues—or people—by disregarding them altogether. It's not that they don't want to succeed; they either don't know how to or are reluctant to get involved out of disinterest or weakness. Some may be wolves in sheep's clothing as well, playing the passive-aggressive card to get what they want by not giving you what you want during the discussion.

How They Operate

Evasive/uncooperative negotiators seek to endure the negotiation without losing. They may be personally insecure or may not feel prepared or knowledgeable about the topic being negotiated. Lack of cooperation and silence for them are survival techniques to avoid saying anything that might be uncomfortable or weaken their position. Or, once again, it can be part of a ploy to gain control through passive-aggressive behavior.

It's easy to get frustrated with this negotiating type as he tends to postpone discussions and to withhold or delay critical information. Issues go unresolved; you may feel that nothing much is being accomplished. Communication may break down or become tense.

Playing Defense

This personality type is difficult; you must diagnose the cause. If the driver is insecurity, try to draw the negotiator out of his shell by reaching out to him and by helping him overcome his fear. If your counterparty has passive-aggressive tendencies, focus on the need to get the task done and make a few concessions to offer some sense of control. Don't withdraw or withhold information yourself; that just keeps the cycle going and may postpone forever the arrival at a successful outcome.

EXPRESSIVE/COMMUNICATIVE

Expressive negotiators exhibit the following traits:

- Playful
- Spontaneous
- Energetic
- Talkative
- Sociable
- Charming
- Self-involved
- A "people person"
- Open
- Easily distracted
- Short attention span
- Enthusiastic
- Think out loud
- Extroverted
- Like being the center of attention
- Ambitious
- Not a good listener
- Like to be reassured

Expressive/communicative negotiators are generally very animated and convey a fun-loving attitude in most situations. They enjoy their work, crave attention, and thrive on rapport. They want to get the negotiation done, feel like they've won, and believe they've entertained you along the way.

How They Operate

Aside from becoming your new best friend, the expressive/communicative negotiators seek to get the most out of the deal by using their social skills and optimism. As such, they may take it personally when you disagree or reject one of their offers. The discussion tends to center on them, sometimes more than the topic being negotiated, and your response and attention—as well as your willingness to do things their way—is their reward.

Instead of conducting business in an even, businesslike tone, expressive/communicative negotiators turn the negotiation into a social function. They may jump from one topic to the next and may be hard to pin down on a particular item. At times they may not let you get a word in edgewise.

Playing Defense

The best way to work with expressive/communicative negotiators is to allow them to do their thing, at least in the beginning. This helps you build rapport. Then, try to keep the negotiation on task with well-timed questions and a focus on the agenda. Don't let them jump around, and don't let them do too much schmoozing. Avoid being too consumed by their charm.

Dealing with Difficult Personalities

Let's face it—we don't get along with everybody, and some people who we have to deal with just flat out rub us the wrong way. What can you do when you just don't mesh well with your counterparty?

The best approach—and I've mentioned this a few times in the Playing Defense subsections—is to try to ignore the unpleasant aspects of your counterparty's personality or style. If he's loud and aggressive, don't respond; stick to business and a normal level of aplomb for the situation. If he's evasive and passive-aggressive, don't take the bait.

Second, and related—stick to business. Focus on the task at hand, on the problem, not the people. Stick to the facts, stick to the agenda. This is part of why it's so important to come *prepared* with the facts and an agenda.

Finally, use the clock effectively. Take time-outs to regroup or to ease the tension. You can use those breaks from the negotiation table to establish some informal rapport with your counterparty so as to diminish some of your differences (which is often easier done in a friendlier, less pressured situation).

The bottom line—and I can't stress it enough—is preparation. Visualize the negotiation, including your response to the difficult personalities you may encounter. And be prepared to separate the people from the problem.

Chapter 5

The Tactical Toolkit: Techniques, Tricks, and Ploys of the Experienced Negotiator

Be it a five-minute or a five-day affair, you're in the final stages of preparing for the negotiation. You've covered all the bases of preparation—visualizing the outcome, preparing the facts, and anticipating the style and tactics of your counterparty. Strategically, you're ready.

Now, as a finalizing stage of your preparation, it's time to review the tactical toolkit. How will you actually go about setting up and making your key points? This chapter explores day-of-the-show tactics, tips, tricks, role plays, and other ploys designed to strengthen your position at the table. These tactical tools—most of them rooted in the principles of behavioral economics—strengthen your position, often by creating subtle emotional responses and overrides on the part of your counterparty. Using these tools will become second nature as you become a more experienced negotiator.

I will share five specific tactical ploys, followed by more general tactical advice for handling specific situations such as not being ready (happens a lot in today's fast-paced world!) and what to do if your position is weak. I should also note that these tactical ploys should be used in moderation. Subtle is best—you don't want to gain the reputation of being a manipulative negotiator. The idea is to manipulate without your counterparty being aware of it. Finally, these tactics are presented—as much else in this book—so that you can see them coming your way as well.

TACTICS—IN CONTEXT

Tricks of the Trade and When to Use Them

Such over-the-table tactics as those I'm about to share are typically deployed—or recognized—in real time. While you may have time to prepare in advance, and while certain situations naturally call for some of these tactics, especially in today's fast-paced world it's even more important to recognize and deal with these tactics and ploys in real time. You won't have a lot of time to analyze; rather, you'll have to know negotiating types and their tactics so well that you can instinctively recognize them as they occur over the board. During a negotiation, you're not studying the pitcher or taking batting practice—you're up at the plate for real.

Honestly—It's about a Win-Win

As mentioned earlier, the best negotiations are win-win—you get what you want, they get what they want; both sides go away with a good relationship that allows for a more effective *next* negotiation. Of course, the double win isn't always possible—some deals end up being more advantageous to one party than the other. But throughout, it always pays to stay as up front and honest as possible. You should strive to avoid becoming the "evil negotiator." Yes, just like you were taught while growing up—honesty is the best policy.

It's okay to use tactical ploys, but don't lie. It will catch up with you, just like it did in your youth. You might get a momentary advantage, but in the long run it will ruin your reputation and make it far more difficult for you to do business.

Now, on to the five tactical ploys.

GOOD COP—BAD COP

Easily recognized in most cases, the good cop–bad cop ploy is a sometimes-entertaining display of two people on the same team playing opposite roles in an effort to distort the counterparty's perception of events and control their emotions. The bad cop is disagreeable—tough minded, unreasonable, maybe irritable and angry. The good cop, on the other hand, is calm and helpful, the peacemaker or collaborator who interjects perhaps to tell the abrasive personality to ease up a little, even creating the impression of helping you.

Surely you've seen this tactic before on TV or in the movies. The bad cop interrogates the murder suspect by screaming, threatening, and bullying. Then the bad cop storms out of the interrogation room only to be replaced by the good cop who befriends the suspect by offering cigarettes, being nice, and promising to help him out of the situation he's in if he would just reveal where the murder weapon is or where the body is buried.

Good Cops and Bad Cops in Business and Personal Settings

In a business setting, the bad cop may drive a hard bargain or set a difficult-to-meet price, while the good cop may suggest a price concession or a concession in another facet of the deal such as service or delivery. Either way, the good cop appears to be mildly on your side, trying to back down the bad cop. It feels good and appeals favorably to our emotions. Behavioral economists have long noted our tendency to accept deals once a higher price, or decoy, is shown. This is because we feel we've gotten a better deal because we've avoided the "bad" one advanced by the bad cop.

You may have witnessed this ploy at a car dealership. The salesperson will play the good cop while his manager, who is never seen, plays the bad cop who won't let the salesperson make any concessions. The salesperson will go back and forth to his manager's office and always come back saying he did everything he could to get what you wanted, but the manager refused to budge. Eventually, he gets something from the manager, or gives you something claimed to be "under the table" as a favor. You're elated because he worked for you, getting you the special perk not available through the bad cop. You thank the salesperson profusely and buy the car.

You may see this in reverse—the manager is the good cop, while the front-line person, in this case the salesperson, is "constrained" by the rules, dealer policy, or some such. The manager comes to the rescue. You're thrilled, even though you probably paid something closer to what the salesperson wanted than you would have liked.

In the household, you see the good cop–bad cop routine all the time, especially when children negotiate with their parents. Dad is the tough guy, Mom comes to the rescue—or vice versa.

Putting Good Cop–Bad Cop Into Play

You can see that this ploy is typically deliberate and planned out in advance as a set of team roles, although it can come forth spontaneously as conditions warrant. You and a team member can slip into good cop and bad cop roles quite naturally if you've done it before. Good cop–bad cop works best when the team members have worked out the bad cop hard line and the good cop concession in advance. Again, though, this can occur quite naturally over the table and can also be an effective way to use a break during which the good cop comes to the rescue.

Counteracting the Good Cop–Bad Cop Ploy

When you encounter this dynamic duo during a negotiation, the bad cop will attempt to intimidate you and is sure to reject every offer you make—perhaps even through animated behavior or by leaving the room in a huff. The good cop then comes to the rescue, appearing to be on your side. It's not hard to identify this tactic, and there are several ways to deal with it:

- Say you want to negotiate with the good cop only.
- Call out the counterparty. Let them know you're onto the ploy.
- Play along. Pretend to be alarmed by the bad cop position and statements. Threaten to end the negotiation. The bad cop may back down, and the good cop may take over.
- Roll out the same ploy. Bring your own bad cop into it. Tell them you'd be more than happy to agree to their demands, but you have a supervisor who never bends the rules. Then come to the rescue as the good cop. If you have the stronger position, your good cop and bad cop will rule the day.
- Speak to the good cop privately. Once alone, tell him you're about to walk away from this negotiation because of the bad cop's behavior, position, or even lack of professionalism. Do it on a break, or give the good cop time to discuss your needs privately with his team.

Dealing with good cops and bad cops, like dealing with all ploys and negotiating tactics, should be fast, friendly, and effective. Getting the bad cop out of the picture early in the game will allow the rest of the negotiation to progress more smoothly.

SHILLS AND DECOYS

In the marketing and selling world, shills are specially placed people who act as bait to lure customers—and in our case, negotiating counterparties. Shills are commonly used in auctions. The shill is a false or fake bidder who is there to put in higher bids. The hope is that you, a legitimate participant, will see the "value" of the item and bid higher. In a casino, you might see someone stationed at a slot machine or table winning over and over. This too-lucky person isn't gambling, he's working for the house.

A decoy is a specially placed, and usually, priced, item that is designed to change your perception of value in the deal. It often comes in the form of a much higher-priced adjacent deal. For example, you see a fine dress shirt for say, $80, and discover one right next to it priced at a mere $50. Such a deal, right? That deal might not look so great if it weren't for the fact that the $80 item was right there next to it. The higher-priced item is designed to make us act emotionally for a moment and snap up the "better" deal. That $80 shirt may have been placed specifically for this purpose, and the retailer may not have any intent to actually sell it.

Decoys psychologically manipulate you away from the true price or value of the deal and may divert your attention away from the real issues. In a negotiation, a decoy that falls outside your parameters is designed to make you feel better about taking the offer that lies within them. A decoy may be used in a defensive position: for instance, when you bring up a prior delivery problem or other issues. These things may not have really been problems, but you play them up to induce the counterparty to grant a concession.

Putting Shills and Decoys Into Play

Again, some preplanning and good teamwork are usually prerequisites, although to an experienced negotiating team some may occur on the fly. The shill can consist of "expert" testimony by a current user of the product or service, someone who appears happy (and may well be) with the deal *he* got.

A typical ploy is to position something as a "must" (like a certain price point) when it is really a "want"; the "must" becomes a limit in the counterparty's mind that feels good when you finally move away from it. "Well, okay, I have a $50 dress shirt on the sale table that's almost as good," you might say. In this light, the $50 shirt may seem like a good option when an $80 shirt is the only alternative choice. In such cases, the more expensive shirt is playing the role of decoy.

You've Been "Shilling" and "Decoying" All Your Life

Seasoned negotiators can see through shills and decoys, so it's important to use these tactics strategically and sparingly. The tactic is common and recognizable once you're aware of it.

It's fun to practice using shills and decoys in your business and on your friends—as I'm sure you've been doing all your life. You got Dad to buy you that bike by finding one less expensive than the one you originally said you wanted (decoy); you got Mom to drop the punitive action by telling her about something good that happened at school (decoy) or by bringing up the kid down the street who didn't get into trouble for doing the same thing (shill).

Fast forward: you run a lawn service and price out a $250 once-a-week do-everything service in hopes of signing the prospective customer up for a once-every-two-weeks service for $150 (decoy). You got a neighbor to come over and thank you for doing such a good job just as you started your sales pitch (shill). Or you got your spouse to settle for a more expensive trip by arranging dinner parties with any number of friends who you knew would testify to their great experience with you (another shill).

A clothing salesperson may use accessories, shoes, or adjacent items as decoys: "Oh by the way, I've got some great ties and shoes on sale over here." Such a statement is designed to give you, the customer, a stronger sense of the value for the deal overall. It also diverts your focus away from the main topic—the $80 shirt and its high price. If the sideline deals really are good, you might get a good feeling from those deals. As a result, you might be more willing to fork over $80 for the dress shirt.

Car salespeople use shills and decoys all the time. You'll hear about a higher-priced model only so that you will feel good about the one in your price range. A sales team associate may show up to tell you how she just sold the higher-priced model to a couple "just like you." You'll be "decoyed off," or seduced, by discussions of floor mats, free service, even free coffee and popcorn at the dealership—all to take your mind off the deal at hand or to make you feel just a little bit better about that deal.

Counteracting the Shill and Decoy

The best way to play defense against this ploy is to see it coming. See "experts" and "expert testimonies" for what they really are. Evaluate each deal or price point based on its own merits. Try not to be overly influenced by the adjacent deal. See decoys for what they are—sophisticated distractions and emotional appeals to get you away from your normal sense of economic value.

Again, Be Honest

A shill can be a clever tactic—or simply a lie. For example, in an interview don't sell yourself to a potential employer by getting a colleague to testify to your exceptional thirty-year career if you haven't worked there for thirty years and your career hasn't been exceptional. While the true number, twenty-five years, will still appear attractive to them, your interview won't be enhanced by the thirty-year claim—instead it will label you as dishonest. And don't try to use a $250 lawn service package—or dire warnings about the imminent death of the lawn—to sell the $150 "mainstream" package if you don't really have a $250 package and the lawn is doing just fine. People figure this out pretty quickly.

When a decoy proves to be a lie or a shill proves to be a liar, that's bad for everyone, and it will become ever harder for all involved to escape the repercussions.

THE STRAW MAN TECHNIQUE

The straw man technique is a ploy to make the counterparty believe something has more value than it really does. The counterparty induces a concession because a negotiating point appears to be important, even though that's not the case. It is similar to a decoy but more likely to be conceived and put into play during the course of the negotiation rather than thought out beforehand.

The best way to explain this ploy is by example. Suppose that during the negotiation to buy a house you decide you would like to include the washer and dryer in the deal. The sellers recognize an opportunity since they were planning to buy a new washer and dryer and leave the old ones anyway. But now they have some additional bargaining power because they know you want them. Rather than simply saying, "Sure. We didn't want to take them with us anyway," they display concern about letting these machines go and say, "Well, maybe ... if you're willing to throw in a couple hundred extra toward our closing costs." They've made an apparent concession to you, but in fact they've used the washer and dryer as a straw man—a feature or item of little value to them—to extract a concession from you.

The element of time can be another straw man. A fabricated or unnecessary delay can be used to get something else of value: "That concession you're asking for will take some time to evaluate—we can reach a deal now if you're willing to withdraw the request." In this case, the saving of time is thrown out as a straw man to move the deal forward—the counterparty really doesn't need extra time to make the decision.

Putting the Straw Man Into Play

Most straw man opportunities will appear as "over-the-board"—that is, at the negotiating table in real time—items that can be made seemingly important to get the other party to reconsider or make a concession. They are difficult to plan for in advance unless you know in advance (through preparation) that an item, like the washer/dryer, will be important, by, say, having their real-estate agent talk to theirs or some such. Don't overuse straw men. The tactic is a stretch of the truth, if not an outright lie, to gain power in the negotiation. If you use it repeatedly and the counterparty figures out the pattern, your straw men will become ineffective; worse, they'll label you as dishonest and manipulative.

Playing Defense

One defense against the straw man tactic is to return the favor. The buyer might say, "You're taking the washer and dryer to your new home? Well, I would like the Sub-Zero fridge" (you really don't, but it's a tactic to get them to reconsider their position on the washer and dryer). Give them alternatives: "If you leave the washer/dryer, it will be so much less work." Or: "You need more time to decide? How can I help you reach the decision more quickly?" You can also ask questions about motives and call their bluff: "Were you really planning to take that old washer and dryer to the new house? The new ones are so much better."

TAKEN BY SURPRISE

No doubt you've experienced this one in your personal life if not in your professional one: An unexpected twist in the negotiation throws you off guard and switches you from relying on facts to reacting based on emotion. From there, concessions can be more easily forthcoming!

In an otherwise smooth discourse, the counterparty suddenly shifts the message or tactics, bringing up new information or displaying a surprising new behavior in hopes of arousing an emotional response or reaction from you. You're caught off guard and often put on the defensive. You see this tactic in TV courtroom dramas all the time.

Don't Be Surprised

Expect a certain amount of surprise, and try to "see" your way through it in advance. Mentally prepare yourself for surprises by visualizing your response and your efforts to redirect the focus back to the negotiation. A surprise that you anticipate and deal with effectively isn't a surprise.

Putting "Taken by Surprise" Into Play

Let's reverse roles and make you the person taking your counter-party by surprise. You throw out a surprise negotiating point ("Did you know that we're about to make the last production run on the widget you're looking to order?") or show a little frustration or anger about a point that she's making. The intent is to break her concentration, put her on the defensive, knock her off balance, or even put her into a panic if she really depends on your widgets. Once her guard is down, it will be easier for you to ask for what you want, if for no other reason than to put the negotiation back on track. This tactic is particularly effective in the case of conflict avoiders.

Playing Defense

If someone tries to take you by surprise:

- Do not react. Since that's exactly what the other party is hoping for, do not give in to the ploy. Stay calm and show your professionalism.
- Take a break. Give yourself time to cool off or to let the new information sink in.
- Ask for details. Learn as much as you can about the new information you've just been given, and determine if it's truly something to be worried about.
- Call for help. If the other party introduces new information to the negotiation and you're not prepared to handle it, convene your team to discuss how to handle the new information.

Dealing with a Surprise Absence

Sometimes the surprise can take the form of the absence of a critical counter-party team member or supervisor. The team sends another person to take his place. This new person may then (intentionally or unintentionally) wear you out with requests for information and to be brought up to speed. The hope is that you'll be thrown off balance or even induced to "help" this replacement—and be more likely to give concessions just to get things going again.

When this happens, keep your composure and stay focused on the goals and main points of the negotiation. Focus on the process, not the people. If necessary you can suggest waiting until the original negotiator is available again. Don't let unplanned absences put you off guard.

ADD-ONS AND NIBBLING

Add-ons and nibbling are two commonly used tactics you'll see over and over. An add-on is a small incremental point or concession that a negotiator adds to the end of a larger concession that's already being discussed. For example, "I'll buy your product if you throw in a free one-year warranty." Nibbling is a variant of the add-on, usually saved for the end of the negotiation, the "one last thing" asked for after a mutually beneficial agreement is reached.

The tactic usually works and is used in both directions in the negotiation. It works because the size of the request is typically small enough that neither party wants to let it derail the agreement. In the case of nibbling, the timing is such that nobody wants to reopen the negotiation. Some negotiators are simply not happy unless they ask for and receive a couple of small concessions. Negotiate much with your kids? You'll see a lot of add-ons and nibbling, some of which is ego driven—just the same as with adults.

Putting Add-Ons and Nibbling Into Play

Add-ons and nibbling are part of the game and can be used to make your win a little sweeter. However, like most ploys, they only work if used sparingly—if you add on heaps of requests, your counterparty will bolt and you may have to start over. Subtle and sweet is best; not too much or too obvious, and always with plenty of manners and grace. Don't let add-ons or nibbling get in the way of the win-win.

Add-ons and nibbles can be calculated in advance or planned over-the-board as conditions warrant. If you sense from your preparation or from the early stages of the negotiation that the counterparty is wary of giving one-year warranties, save that point for the end or add it to a larger concession you're making. Doing so will preserve the win-win feeling.

Playing Defense

The best defense is to recognize the add-on or nibble for what it is—a ploy and an adjunct to the main agreement designed to bring a little more satisfaction to the other party. Evaluate it quickly, and if it's not too costly for you, go ahead and accept the add-on as a cost of doing business, part of the price for achieving the win-win. If the add-ons and nibbles get too large or numerous, call out your counterparty, and get him to back off. Don't be afraid to request to stop and re-enter the negotiation if necessary. You can also throw a few add-ons and nibbles of your own into the fray.

Some Concessions Are More
Equal Than Others

Just because a concession sounds small or comes up as a minor amendment at the end, don't assume that it is. Take the time to appraise it objectively—don't let the emotional need to preserve the deal or conclude the negotiation force you into oversized add-on or nibble concessions. Keep to your agenda, goals, and objectives.

A SHORT LIST OF OTHER TACTICS

Other Ploys to Prepare For

Here are a few other common negotiating tricks and ploys you'll see—and may use—from time to time:

- *Funny money.* Funny money is real money presented in a way that makes it seem less real. When gambling, you exchange cash for chips, a tactic casinos employ to make customers feel as if they're not gambling with real money. In negotiating, the other party may use funny money—barter, nonmonetary concessions. They may even phrase things in percentages or points instead of dollars to shift your focus away from cost or price.
- *Red herring.* A red herring is a glaring decoy or straw man. A negotiator might enter a negotiation with a *huge* request—a ten-year warranty—in hopes of getting a one-year warranty or some other major concession. He never expected the ten-year warranty in the first place, but he did want to change the balance of power in the negotiation.
- *Low-balling.* You may hear a one-time offer or concession that goes away as you get into the details of the negotiation. You hear a great price, but then start to hear about the various conditions ("Well, that price is only good on the first Tuesday after a full moon"). But now you're hooked.
- *Flinching.* A variant of Taken by Surprise, a counterparty throws an "out-of-the-ballpark" price or term into the agreement just to gauge your reaction. You flinch—and the degree of your flinch is

used as the starting point to find something you can agree on. Of course, you can work the idea in reverse: You can use a flinching response to feign surprise to keep the counterparty off balance, even if you perceive her offer as fair or close to fair.

- *Crunch.* The negotiator—particularly the intimidator—uses this tactic to make you doubt your position by rejecting your entire offer, using terms like, "You'll have to do much better than that" or "That's just not good enough for me." The counterparty uses the crunch to gain power and keep you off balance. He may be trying to make you feel fortunate that you're able to make a different offer. To defend against this tactic, ask a lot of "why" questions about the reasons the terms you've proposed aren't good enough; you may find that the objections to them disappear quickly.
- *Bogey.* A bogey is used as a third-party scapegoat, some kind of immovable object that prevents flexibility in a deal. As an example, the counterparty might blame her manager or some internal rule for why she cannot bring down certain fees. When you detect a bogey, ask a lot of questions or even to speak to the person if it is a person. If it's a rule, ask to read the rule. Get to the authority behind the bogey when you can.

WHAT TO DO WHEN YOU'RE THE UNDERDOG

How to Acquire Leverage

Aside from the specific tactics described in the previous sections, it is helpful to carry some more general strategies and tactics in your negotiator's toolkit for dealing with situations when the balance of power is decidedly not in your favor.

Negotiating power is dependent on a number of components, all of which work together to create the leverage you can use during the negotiation. Ideally both sides have more or less equal bargaining power. That said, it's common to perceive that one side has more of it than the other. Both sides typically have strengths and weaknesses that can be used to their advantage to create win-win solutions that work across the table. In the real world, however, for a variety of reasons you might find yourself in a position of unequal power or leverage.

Suppose the other party has a prestigious reputation, is a long-acknowledged expert on the topic, has superior negotiating skills, and has a stellar team backing him up. You have none of these advantages, making you the underdog in the negotiations. You can still do well, but you'll need to prepare more. Here are some tactics to deal with being an underdog:

- Recognize the situation. Don't be intimidated by those credentials—they don't ultimately affect the win-win.
- Figure out where you can acquire leverage. Bring in experts of your own, take a careful inventory of your capabilities and

find a unique value proposition different from the competition. Look at all aspects of what you're trying to deliver or do for your counterparty—price, quality, service, protection, brand, sustainability, ease of doing business—and determine your strengths especially compared to the competition.

- Research what you don't know. If lack of knowledge about the issues makes you the underdog, take it upon yourself to bridge the gap. Do some quick research. Hit the Internet. Tap your social and professional network. Learn what you can as quickly as you can; become an "instant expert."

- Be confident. Walk into the negotiation as if you couldn't possibly fail. Don't cave—no matter how strong or unpleasant your counterparty might turn out to be. Standing firm shifts the balance of power right off the bat. It may take a little acting, but projecting confidence will help you both in the near term and in the long run.

IF YOU'RE NOT READY

Simply put, if you're not ready to negotiate, don't. Maybe you need more time to prepare, or maybe you need more information from the other party; whatever the reason, do what you can to avoid putting yourself in a position you'll regret later. Let your counterparty know as soon as possible that you're not ready; see if you can agree on another date. Offer an alternative and be as precise as possible so the counterparty doesn't get the impression you're procrastinating.

If you need additional information from the other party, ask them to provide it. Explain how these details will help you resolve the conflict that's holding back your prep.

If the situation is difficult, remember the win-win paradigm—you want to win, and the other party deserves to win, too. Remind your counterparty of this philosophy. You should give—and ask for—enough time to prepare to come to the table with a reasonable and equal chance to win. If he can't live up to this principle, then he may not be fit to do business with in the long term anyway.

CASE STUDY

Once you've silenced the intimidating CEO of client firm Dewey and Cheatum in your pitch to make Filmographic Productions their exclusive supplier of video services, your challenges aren't over. You may have done well with Cheatum, the good cop, but Dewey, the bad cop, is still intent on beating down your offer to what he considers a better deal. To match him, you'll have to deploy some tactics.

You might keep talking to Cheatum the good cop. You might bring your own good cop, say, your video editor, or even your spouse, who keeps the books and runs the business, into the equation. You might even try (this is hard!) being both good and bad cop by taking a tougher stance, then backing down a bit to make your opponent feel a bit of a victory.

You might try a shill in the form of a testimonial or even a live appearance by a similar client. Anything to make Cheatum and especially Dewey feel good about your work or even spark a competitive fire ("Well, my competitor got this really great commercial from Filmographic? I'm gonna get one too!") might work to your advantage. You could offer a decoy, such as a higher valued high-definition segment at a high price, but then tell them they don't need such a high-definition production for what they're trying to accomplish—so the cost will be much less.

As you move further into the negotiations, you can employ a wider range of tactics. Straw men can come into play. After all, photographers and videographers have lots of good tactics to throw out. "On location" sounds expensive and valuable, but in reality most videographers would rather work in the client's location than hire one out and adapt it to the script. Similarly, copies of the video can have more perceived value than their actual cost to produce, and so can be used as easy concessions throughout. You could also offer some other shots of their business premises "for free" because you're already on location.

The more straw men you can throw out there, the more cooperative and supportive you will appear to be, even though these straw men don't represent much of a concession to you. You may surprise them with an extra charge to rent the latest fancy camera equipment, then rescind the charge because you were going to use that more-expensive equipment anyway and add something else to the agreement to cover the cost of using it. Alternatively, you could back off on the special fee, using the element of surprise to make the client more amenable to a higher overall fee.

Travel fees, editing fees, and rental and other fees can all be slipped in as add-ons or nibbles toward the close of the negotiation. If you've made your pitch well throughout the negotiation and the client feels an overall win is at hand, you'll get some of these concessions and win a little more yourself.

But again, don't overdo these tactics and ploys. You might end up making a bad movie, and nobody wants a producer who has a reputation for making bad movies.

Among the earliest forms of currency were cowrie shells. They were used to facilitate the exchange of goods and services in China more than 3,000 years ago. Gradually such means of exchange, a fundamental element in economic negotiations, were replaced by coins fashioned from gold and silver.

Top: The remains of the Roman Forum where citizens of the Republic negotiated everything from trade agreements to marriages to land purchases. Nearby, the Senate met, where the wealthiest citizens negotiated about the Republic's laws and treaties.

Bottom: One of the most important negotiations in American history occurred in Philadelphia in 1781 when delegates from the former thirteen colonies hammered out the constitution of a new country: the United States of America. Among the points on which they negotiated were slavery, proportional representation of different states, and the duties and powers of the President.

Top: John F. Kennedy said, "Let us never negotiate out of fear. But let us never fear to negotiate." Among the most important negotiated treaties of Kennedy's presidency was the 1963 Partial Test Ban Treaty between the United States and the Soviet Union, which limited the testing of nuclear weapons.

Bottom: The Vietnam War formally ended in 1975 after many years of negotiations. The Paris Peace Accords, the treaty that brought the war to a close, won Nobel Peace prizes for Dr. Henry Kissinger, national security advisor to the President of the United States, and Lê Đức Thọ, chief negotiator for Vietnam. Today, the war and its victims are commemorated in many memorials such as the one seen here.

Opposite page top: The United Nations offers one forum in which many international negotiations take place. The UN often acts as a mediator in disputes between countries, ranging from trade and commerce to conflicts about borders. **Opposite page bottom:** The Federal Trade Commission, a government agency that focuses on consumer protection, was created by Congess in 1914. It mandates that in the purchase of a large-ticket item (for instance, a house), the buyer has three days in which to change her mind. Federal and state laws can sometimes affect the terms or outcome of negotiations. **This page:** President Theodore Roosevelt, a formidable negotiator, offered this advice to those negotiating on behalf of the American government: "Speak softly, and carry a big stick." In other words, Roosevelt advised avoiding bluster but instead exercising power firmly and fairly. Roosevelt received a Nobel Prize for his efforts in mediating an end to the Russo-Japanese War in 1905.

A "red herring" is a distraction that's brought into a negotiation in the hopes of making one party lose its focus. The term possibly originated when the nineteenth-century radical William Cobbett, who was opposed to hunting, used herring to distract dogs from the smell of the fox. Since then it's come to mean anything that deliberately draws someone in the wrong direction.

A common negotiation that most people will go through at some point in their lives is buying a car. It's one of the only large purchases (another is a house) in which the price of what is being bought and sold is negotiable. Haggling over the car price is often one of the biggest negotiations people undertake.

Among the biggest business negotiations of the early twenty-first century was the 2000 merger between AOL and Time Warner. The merger created one of the largest media companies in the world (its headquarters shown here) and was widely hailed at the time as a business coup. However, due to a lack of clarity in the negotiations followed by poor execution, the company experienced many difficulties, and AOL spun off as a separate company in 2009.

The end result of a business negotiation will probably be a contract. The party that writes the contract is generally considered to have an advantage, since this allows control over the document's phrasing. Both parties, by their signatures, indicate that they understand and agree to the terms arrived at through negotiation.

Chapter 6

Pure Theater: Negotiating on Stage

In the last chapter, we examined some of the more common tactics and ploys a negotiator might use to appeal to the emotions of a counterparty and distract him or her from what might be the most prudent course of action. Those ploys were primarily in substance and not in presentation or "stagecraft." In this chapter we explore the pure "theater" of action, the verbal and visual tactics a negotiator might deploy. A counterparty might intentionally use theatrics to throw you a little off balance and gain an edge, or subconsciously use them to the same effect. As is always the case, you can do more than just recognize and defend against these tactics; you can also be clever in your day-of-the-show stagecraft and put them into play to achieve your own goals and outcomes.

I'll cover several verbal and visual negotiation tactics in this chapter so that you can recognize them for what they are: theatrics. I should note that these ploys have more power during a face-to-face negotiation than in an electronic negotiation. Nonetheless, the principles of these tactics still apply. Put the playbills down, dim the lights, and let's get on with the show!

PLAYING DUMB

Knowing More Than They Think You Do

You, or your counterparty, may choose to "play dumb"—that is, appear to be less informed or prepared than you are—to appeal to the ego of a counterparty or to find out more information. Instead of risking an uncomfortable confrontation by coming right out with "Why did your production department fail to meet its yearly quota?" you might play dumb instead and ask for this year's numbers and compare them to last year's.

You already know the answer, but by playing dumb you made the other party feel less defensive. The counterparty may begin to believe that you don't know that they missed their quota, and this may give them a false sense of confidence that they know more than you do. They may also be more willing to tell you more about the decline in numbers. Playing dumb is a way to fish for more and to keep your fish biting.

This tactic may allow you to confirm information you already know. You may also know the answer, but playing dumb gives you a chance to assess how forthright your counterparty is; you'll be able to assess how well their answer matches what you already know.

WHEN YOUR COUNTERPARTY PLAYS DUMB

If you start to sense a lot of "beating around the bush" questions, your counterparty might be playing dumb, waiting for you to make a mistake. If you feel that your counterparty is digging excessively, that his playing dumb is a tactic designed just to trip you up, then you need to end the inquiries. You aren't on trial. The best approach is to call him out: Ask right away if there's a deeper issue he would like to talk about, and try to determine where his questions are going. It may simply be that he needs the information and doesn't have it on hand.

Occasionally you can defuse a playing dumb scenario by using the same tactic yourself. If you sense unnecessary questioning designed to trick you into a mistake or to artificially build your ego, you can do the same thing. Simply ask open-ended questions about something you already know. Doing so can buy you time to figure out your next steps. It often pays to know more about a topic than you lead your counterparty to believe.

From the Playbook of Socrates

The Greek philosopher Socrates taught his students how to logically think about and argue the statements they made. To do so he engaged them in a philosophical debate, ultimately drawing them into a contradiction of their original statement. By actively participating in the debate, the students learned to think for themselves. Eventually they learned to see through the trap of Socrates's questioning.

When you feel as if the Socratic method is in play—that is, unending leading questions designed to manipulate you into a trap—stop! Redirect every question to a main objective, asking how the question pertains to the goals you are both trying to reach. Explain that you don't want to waste time on unending trivial inquiries that don't lead to solutions. Keep your answers short to deflect further questioning.

BE THE INTERROGATOR

The Power of Asking Questions

Questions are an important part of any conversation, and negotiations in particular. Questions serve many functions. Most are aboveboard attempts to get facts and "soft" factors—the often-nuanced background, experience, or culture *behind* the facts—but some questions conceal a hidden agenda. The art of formulating and framing questions, often done on the fly, is important to negotiating success. Learning to recognize various question types will help you be able to put together skillful, suitably targeted questions—and you'll learn to recognize hidden agendas in questions headed your way.

I'll describe three types of questions you need to be familiar with: vague, loaded, and leading. You've fielded them all, no doubt, and have also posed each type a time or two.

VAGUE QUESTIONS

Vague questions are just as they sound—they don't lead to a specific answer. As such, they can prompt unexpected responses. If the other party asks vague questions, it's easy to misinterpret what they really mean—and you might give an answer you did not intend to disclose. For example, the question, "How accurate is that figure?" is a vague question dressed up in superficial specifics. Think about possible answers you might give, and you'll soon realize there are few if any specific answers. You might reply with, "Fairly accurate," "highly accurate," or even "100 percent accurate." Regardless, these aren't specific answers; they are vague answers. But in giving them, you indicate some ambiguity in the figure, which invites further discussion that in turn may cause you to reveal something you didn't intend to be known.

"Are you having a good day?" is another vague question—how? Personally? Professionally? Seems innocent, but it's a vague question that may evoke either a vague answer or a specific answer you don't really want to give.

To counteract vague questions, simply ask for more specifics. "Does that figure look right to you? Does it seem too high or too low?" "Are you asking about my work day so far?" If your counterparty is using vague questions to fish for information and unexpected answers, get exact details about what she wants to know before giving too much away.

LOADED QUESTIONS

More ingenious and dangerous than the vague question is the loaded question. A loaded question is more like a judgment wrapped up in a nice package topped off with a question mark bow. It sounds like you're being asked a question, but you're really being led to a conclusion—usually a negative one. For example, "Is your staff still disorganized?" Either way you answer it, you're trapped in a negative conclusion. "Yes" is obviously negative; "no" admits it was disorganized earlier.

Loaded questions force you to admit something negative with any possible answer. Careful listening will help you identify loaded questions. Once again, the way to deflect these attacks is to ask for clarification or a reframing of the question before answering.

When to Answer a Question with a Question

If you answer a loaded question right away, you validate the question and the negative position it implies. If you answer a question like, "Is your staff still disorganized?" right away, you're pretty much admitting that you agree the staff was disorganized, meaning that the only remaining issue at hand is whether it is *still* disorganized.

So the best way to handle this question is not to answer it directly. You can instead answer the question with another question. "When did you see any evidence of my staff being disorganized?" or "When is the last time you spent any time with my staff?"

The shoe will shift to the other foot. Now your interrogator is on the defensive.

LEADING QUESTIONS

Lawyers use leading questions frequently, and when they do, an objection from the opposing lawyer is usually quick to follow. A leading question tries to get a specific response, usually to prove the asker's point.

Examples of leading questions in a negotiation might be, "This price is really high, isn't it?" or "Isn't your delivery schedule substantially slower than those of your competitors?" or "Your firm has had a lot of quality control issues in the past, hasn't it?" You can see how these questions, as structured, target a particular response.

One feature of many leading questions is the interrogative tacked on at the end: "isn't it?" "doesn't it?" or "don't you?" and so on. A question followed by such a sub-question is often leading.

In the courtroom, a leading question may be used to create a dramatic presentation for the jury. The opposing lawyer objects to a leading question because it tries to trick the witness into agreeing. Typically the lawyer already knows the answers to the questions—he knows the script and is using the witness as his unknowing sidekick.

If you think the counterparty is using leading questions to prove a point, remind him politely that you are not on trial and that you would like to save time by discussing issues objectively. Or answer the question as if it had been structured as nonleading: "How does your delivery schedule compare to that of your competitors?"

The More They Talk, the Less They Say

Some people use talking as a way to compensate for what they lack in negotiating position strength. The less they have to offer, the more they talk to compensate for their deficiencies.

WHEN THEY TALK TOO MUCH

Getting Through the Gab

A well-balanced discussion involves an equal amount of talking and listening among all parties. All negotiators want to feel that what they're saying is important to the rest of the table. When given the chance, however, some people tend to dominate the conversation or discussion by talking too much. Sometimes this is intentional; sometimes the person doesn't realize how much he's talking. All negotiations have a rhythm of give and take and of talk and listen. Excessive talking can throw you and the negotiation off course.

Are You Talking Too Much?

If you realize that you're the chatty culprit, stop, apologize for controlling the conversation, and graciously give up the floor. Acknowledging your mistake will help regain the rhythm of the negotiation and make you right with the crowd. If others are too chatty, you can politely ask them to "take the conversation into the parking lot" or some such phrase.

Reasons for Rambling

Rambling can be part of a negotiating style, and the more you read the signals the better you can guess the intentions. A ramble can be either deliberate or purely accidental. Here is a quick field guide.

Deliberate rambling signs include:

- Denies the opportunity for someone else to interject with comments or questions, even when you signal that you have something to add.
- Shrugs off your comments and questions, or says, "Let's talk about that later."
- Interrupts when it's your turn to speak.

Accidental rambling signs include:
- Repeats thoughts, speaks quickly, and uses a lot of run-on sentences, a possible sign of nervousness and insecurity.
- Makes a lot of jokes and aimless chitchat; although it may seem this person is avoiding the issues, these could be an attempt to make a good impression or to establish rapport. He seems to crave attention.
- Fills silences by talking about more concerns or goals; this person may be uncomfortable with long periods of silence or could be thinking out loud.

Sweet Talk? Or Information Overload?

Excessive talk can be used as a tactic to bombard you with so much information that you miss the important points. The counterparty may give you all the pertinent facts up front and then deliver a deluge of information causing you lose focus. This ploy will overwhelm you with so much data that you forget the questions you had about the real issues, fail to notice erroneous assumptions, and miss the chance to inquire about gray areas.

It can be difficult to get straight answers from ramblers. The longer the answer, the harder it becomes to extract the information you need. If necessary, repeat the question (and the answer!) until you are clear about the real answer. If the other person tries to evade the question with doublespeak, keep pressing.

A SHOUTING MATCH

Dealing with Loud Outbursts

Few dramatic moments perk up one's ears more than being shouted at. Shouting makes us feel uneasy or even embarrassed, especially if others can hear. Shouters know this and may choose to use this discomfort to their advantage.

There are different reasons for shouting. We shout out of fear ("What will the boss think if I don't bring back this deal?"), out of aggression ("I'm telling you loud and clear why this is important!"), or as an attempt to manipulate, keeping the counterparty off balance and insecure about how the negotiation is proceeding. Not everyone shouts for the same reason, so listen carefully to what the other party is saying (or shouting) to pick up on the cues.

Generally—as with most other acts of theater—the best countermeasure is to maintain your composure and proceed with professional aplomb. Try to figure out the motive for the shouting by listening carefully (and actively) and asking questions.

Whether the behavior is brought on by stress or is just an act should become clear fairly quickly. Ask for explanations in a diplomatic, calming way; try not to be defensive. If the shouting has arisen from stress (for instance, from a tight deadline), try to help the counterparty work out the causes for the stress (perhaps, by discussing the deadline). Show empathy and remind your counterparty that you seek a win-win.

Don't Shout Back

The worst thing you can do when your counterpart starts shouting—as tempting as it might be—is to shout back. That just gives more reason for the shouting to continue and the situation to escalate. Instead, pause, collect your thoughts, ask a few calming questions, and shift the focus back to a factual discussion. Staying composed, focused on reason and the win-win—rather than emotion—should calm down your counterparty.

OTHER EMOTIONAL OUTBURSTS

From shouting we move to a more general topic of emotional outbursts: acted-out drama designed by some of the better negotiators to get what they want. Not only might you see shouting, you might see staged tears, thinly disguised threats, feigned indifference, or even superiority—the list is long. The purpose of these performances is to tap into your emotions and gain control of your thoughts—and to see how malleable you are. Can you be easily swayed? Or are you focused on the facts and logic of the negotiation?

The best way to deal with such theatrics is to, first, ignore them, and second, to try to get behind them to understand their true meaning. You can take breaks. If the outbursts are severe you can offer to postpone or reschedule the negotiation. Try to get the message across that you aren't likely to respond or give in to theatrical performances. If the emotional outbursts really seem real, use a little empathy to figure out where your counterparty is coming from.

Beware the Emotional Outburst

An explosion of anger is the most common kind of outburst. Sob stories and guilt trips can also be used to make you believe that the situation is worse than it is. You might also see feigned helplessness, where the counterparty wants you to think that he's giving up—and that there's only one thing you can do to get him to come back. Give in.

But remember: If you give in to these acts, they're likely to be used again.

If It Becomes Blatant Abuse

Abuse comes in many forms. The abuser strives to wreak havoc on your ego to achieve her own goals. Abusers use personal attacks to gain control. Verbal abuse—in the form of name-calling, foul language, emotional exploitation, manipulation, and cruelty—is intended to shake your self-confidence and well-being.

If you're feeling abused, stick up for yourself. Stop the negotiation and inform the counterparty that the abusive behavior is unacceptable. If you don't defend yourself, you will lose the respect of the counterparty and the tirade will continue.

THE UNSPOKEN WORD

Body Language

Often the most important part of a face-to-face or video conversation involves no words at all. While psychologists disagree on the exact percentages and maintain that it depends on the situation, the conventional wisdom—at least in a face-to-face context—is that 55 percent of what is actually communicated comes from body language, 38 percent is from tone of voice, and 7 percent is from what is actually said.

These numbers are a powerful reminder that you should observe and read gestures, facial expressions, eye contact, body posture, and the use of space in assessing what your counterparty is trying to say or even what he is feeling at the moment.

Becoming fluent in body language requires time, effort, practice, and application, but it's worth the effort. Body language skills will help you uncover hidden agendas, discover a person's true feelings, gain insight into someone's character, predict reactions, and become aware of your own nonverbal behavior. Following are some guiding principles of body language and behaviors.

BODY LANGUAGE IS SUBCONSCIOUS BEHAVIOR

Most of the time we don't know that our bodies are silently and subconsciously communicating with the rest of the world. Body language is instinctive. People don't consciously move their arms when they speak—it just happens; it's a neurological response to complex inner feelings. It's natural for arms to move, feet to tap, and eyes to turn away when engaged in conversation. In fact, it feels very unnatural to carry out these behaviors consciously.

The challenge of reading body language lies in how misleading it can be. Many nonverbal cues can be interpreted in numerous ways. While there are some generalizations, each signal is unique to the person and the context.

It's useful to observe how body language is used in conjunction with speech. After you gain some experience with this, you'll realize that nonverbal cues can either emphasize the spoken words or undermine them. For example, if a person says he's satisfied with your offer but grips his pen and clenches his fist as he says so, you might ask yourself if he's really unhappy with the offer. To test this assumption, ask a few questions to see if he can open up and tell you how he really feels.

"In Control"—Is It Just an Act?

The ability to control body language is an important part of being an actor. Good actors can suppress natural body language and project an appearance of emotion far different from what they're really feeling. Negotiators who are also good actors can deploy this skillset to their advantage. You can often determine their acting skills by watching their behaviors away from the negotiation—before, after, on breaks, and so forth. Beware—and be aware.

There are more nonverbal cues than I can list, and there are multiple ways to interpret them. The following table gives a useful sample of some of the more common nonverbal cues:

Common Nonverbal Cues	
Body Language	Possible Meaning
Clenched hands, strong grip on object	Frustration
Cocked head	Interested, attentive
Covering mouth with hands	Dishonesty, stretching the truth
Crossed arms	Defensive, immovable, opposing
Crossed legs, ankles	Competitive, opposing
Fidgeting	Apprehensive, unconfident
Finger tapping or drumming	Boredom or apprehension
Frequent nodding	Eagerness
Hand-steepling (forming church)	Confidence
Hands on cheek, chin, or glasses	Thinking, examining
Hands on hips	Confidence, impatience
Hands on table or desk	Poise
Head in hand	Disinterested, disrespectful, or disagreeing
Leaning forward	Enthusiastic
Open arms, hands	Open-minded, approachable
Rubbing nose, forehead	Uptight, confrontational

Common Nonverbal Cues	
Body Language	Possible Meaning
Side glance	Suspicion or uncertainty
Sitting on edge of seat	Prepared, enthusiastic
Slouching, leaning back	Challenging, rejecting
Throat-clearing	Nervousness or impatience

These basic cues are visible and fairly universal. Some, like throat-clearing, can be picked up in an "invisible" situation (for example, when the negotiation is taking place over the phone). But keep in mind that not all human beings do everything the same way, and what might tip the hand of one individual may not necessarily reveal the inner feelings of another.

COMPLEX CUES

Not surprisingly, it gets more complex. Many cues, like facial expressions and vocalization, are more subtle or are combinations of other cues, such as the following.

Facial Expressions

Over the centuries we've developed a wide range of social behaviors, including the resourcefulness of communicating a message with just a single look. As soon as we meet someone for the first time, we begin sizing him up and immediately search for clues that indicate his character before even entering a conversation. Facial expressions are a big part of this initial assessment.

Facial expressions can quickly and easily summarize a person's disposition in real time and can be invaluable "reads" throughout the course of a negotiation. Key facial expressions include raised eyebrows (uncertainty, concern), nose scratching (confusion), widening of the eyes (surprise, disbelief, anxiety), and minor eye squinting (contemplative, questioning). You've seen them all in professional and personal life. As a negotiator, it pays to stop and think about what they mean, and to learn to recognize them for what they are in your interactions.

Vocalization

Your voice is instrumental in expressing how you feel. Tone, tempo, and cadence can be as important if not more important than word choice in communication. Voice can be used to get your point across, to get someone's attention, to soothe or calm nerves, or to gain insight into your counterparty's intentions.

Vocal tone contains many elements: pitch (high or low frequency), stress (emphasis), and volume (loudness), among others. These elements place greater or lesser importance on certain words being spoken and can easily be missed or misinterpreted. Consider the following example, where the boldface words indicate the emphasis:

- **What** do you want?
- What **do** you want?
- What do **you** want?
- What do you **want**?

Note how the meaning of each question is changed depending on where the emphasis is. If it's still unclear, read each one out loud with the appropriate inflection and think about how you would react to each question.

Speak Softly—and Carry a Big Stick

Loud tones can be used to get someone's attention or to make a point, but they may sound threatening and filled with anger and thus detract from the point. Soft, quiet tones make people feel relaxed and safe, and as a result they're more likely to listen to the point. Quiet confidence supported by solid facts ("big stick") rules and invites the win-win. But not *too* quiet—you might signal weakness and be ignored!

Tempo and Cadence

Tempo refers to how fast you speak (rushing through sentences or talking in a slow and calculated manner). Cadence, on the other hand, refers to the rhythm or style of your voice (dull monotone or exciting variations). If your counterpart is speaking too fast, she may be impatient—or worse, nervous or apprehensive. If her voice drones on without any use of inflection, tone, or pitch, she may not care or may be distracted. But don't go too far with these assessments. Tempo and cadence may simply be part of a person's speaking style and may not be indicative of the current situation. Again, an "offline" assessment during breaks or outside the negotiation may reveal the true speaking style.

The Advantages and Dangers of Electronic Negotiating

In today's connected world, nonverbal communication can still transcend the actual words used, although not as easily. Texts or email messages can have a tone as well—they can be very short and curt and to the point, one word, even; or they can be friendly, glib, and explanatory. Because of the usually minimal effort to produce these messages, especially text, you shouldn't read too much into terse messages. But still, you can pick up some clues, especially if a person sends friendlier messages at other times or is friendly in person. If in doubt, you can send a friendly message; if the return message is still curt, you might be contending with a detached or annoyed counterparty.

Reading between the lines is something we all do, all the time, no matter the medium.

DEALING WITH—AND USING—BODY LANGUAGE

Reading the Cues

Body language is subconscious and innate for most of us; it is an integral part of who we are. While it's important to realize that some of it can be controlled, for the most part it is natural. As such it is a valuable window into someone's true meanings and intentions in a negotiation.

You can't really defend against body language; the best defense is to be aware and recognize it for what it is. Short of being a talented actor, you can also use body language—and in some cases modify it slightly—to help achieve your communication goals.

Mirroring Your Counterparty

Here's an effective way to build trust with the other party: Repeat her style of speaking, writing, emailing, texting, tone of voice, and posture. If done with skill (without seeming to mock her) your counterparty will feel understood, and you'll have established a foundation for open communication.

Don't imitate, but try to use familiar and comfortable communication styles where it makes sense.

People naturally have a tendency to favor one sense over another—their visual sense, their auditory sense, or their sense of or need for structure. Use the following emphasis (really, a nonverbal communication *style*) when you sense that someone falls into one of these categories:

- *The visual thinker.* People who prefer to understand their world from a mostly visual perspective respond to color, shapes, graphic design elements, and physical movements. They tend to like pictures, draw pictures themselves, and sometimes make statements like, "It seems clear from my point of view," and "I see where you're coming from." Try to use visual forms of communication where possible, and you may want to incorporate visual elements into your own speech: "It looks good to me."

- *The auditory thinker.* These individuals are attuned to a world of sounds. They tend to hear before they see, and they recall memories by first describing the sounds they remember during that moment in time. They are keen on observing tone and the sounds of movement (slamming doors, sighs of frustration). Their statements include, "It sounds good to me," "I hear what you're saying," and "I don't have to listen to this." Make sure your auditory cues are clear and perceptible.

- *The structural thinker.* Some need to see—or hear—the structure in everything you're talking about. Your presentation should be visually or audibly structured so they can see the elements of a fact, a statement, or a conclusion. Structured discussions should include plenty of road signs: "First, X, second, Y, then last, Z." Such an approach will help this thinker process what you're saying and where you're going.

READING AND SENDING
APPROPRIATE SIGNALS

As you can see, body language can be challenging to master. You really need to observe the context, the whole picture, to get a true read at times. And it's easy to misinterpret. Reading body language can be guesswork; no one can ever be 100 percent sure of someone's true intentions or meaning. Nevertheless, a few techniques and tests can help you recognize patterns and inconsistencies in the counterparty as well as within yourself.

The Body Language Pretest

At the beginning of a negotiation, you and your counterparty will usually exchange friendly chat to build rapport and get to know each other. During this process, you'll get to know his nonverbal personality as well. Look for breathing patterns, facial expressions, smiles (and what kind of smiles—friendly or sarcastic smirk); listen for tone; and watch eye contact. Once you've committed these impressions to memory, use them as a reference point once negotiations begin.

Put on a Happy Face—And Get Your Counterparty to Do the Same

One technique to decipher body language is to get your counterparty to talk about something he's happy about—like his significant other, children, pets, or cars. Since he's not pretending to be happy about his favorite things, you can note his body language while he's talking about Fluffy, and then look for those "happy" cues later in the negotiation.

Who's Bluffing?

The best way to tell if someone is bluffing during a negotiation is to ask questions. If you recognize nonverbal cues (shiftiness, nervousness, suddenly disappeared eye contact) suggesting that your counterpart is bluffing, poke around a little. Ask her to back up her statements if you see that her body language is not quite consistent with what she is saying.

Look in the Mirror

It helps to understand *your own* body language. If you want to be sure you're sending the right signals, videotape yourself giving a couple of talks (even if it's a birthday speech or toast to your best friend) and review the tape. Watch your own nonverbal behaviors, then ask colleagues, friends, or even family how they perceive your body language. Once you know these subconscious cues, you can work on developing your very own poker face.

Silence Can Be Golden: Using and Interpreting Silence

Twentieth-century French composer Claude Debussy summed up the power of silence beautifully: "Music is the silence between the notes." Silence can change or alter a conversation dynamic in many subtle ways.

Silence can be an important tool in keeping control of the discussion, or in giving others (or yourself) time to think. The presence of silence causes many of the more extroverted among us to become uncomfortable—someone must always be saying something, right? In such a scenario, the extrovert might "fill the hole" in the discussion by revealing more than he should.

Silence is also a great way to give your counterparty a chance to voice something he's been waiting for the right moment to say. After you've made your pitch, "go silent" to induce him to make his. He'll appreciate that you're not trying to monopolize the conversation. Say nothing, and let it happen.

Silence can also be used to put pressure on the other party. It can put him on the spot, and again induce an unprepared or off-target response. By going silent, you may be able to get the counterparty to relinquish a power position—of course, subconsciously. The counterparty probably doesn't realize he is being put on the spot.

All that said, be careful not to use (or tolerate) too much silence—you might come off as passive-aggressive and thus untrustworthy. Other "talkers" might chime in and throw the meeting off course, or others might get the idea you're not interested. As with all other tools, ploys, and tactics, use silence sparingly; don't be obvious.

CASE STUDY

Listening to Unspoken Language

As a representative of Filmographic Productions, you're halfway through your discussions with Dewey and Cheatum about becoming their exclusive supplier of video services. You've pushed back the attacks of the intimidator, a role played by CEO Cheatum. And by being aware of the good cop–bad cop routine, you've been able to play off one executive against another. Through your use of straw men you've made some concessions, like on-location filming, that are not really significant to you but that sound big to the other side.

As the discussion continues, you notice that one of Dewey's negotiators is sitting hunched in his chair, silent and apparently half ignoring the discussions around him. Arms folded and legs crossed, he's staring intently at a piece of paper on the table in front of him, doodling—not taking notes about what's been discussed.

Everything about this man screams "No!" He looks deeply unhappy, as if Dewey were about to jump off a cliff. You aren't the only one watching him; other Dewey negotiators are aware of him as well, and his closed attitude seems to be affecting the discussion, which gradually subsides.

Clearly you're going to have to win over this man. But before deciding how, you take a quick inventory of your own body language:

- Are your arms or legs crossed?
- Are you meeting others' gazes directly?
- Are you frequently covering your mouth or touching some other facial feature?
- Are you slouching in your chair?

If you've been doing any of these, you've been sending the wrong signals to your counterparties. Remember that you seek a win-win negotiation; and you're not going to accomplish that if they think you're sullen, resentful, or holding something back.

Having identified a barrier by correctly reading body language, you deploy tactics to bring the recalcitrant Dewey executive on board. You open up to him, physically and verbally. You ask questions to find out if he understands your proposal and if he's on board or not. You listen. You deploy some silence to give him a chance to talk. You remind him of the win-win objective. All for one—then one for all—you keep the negotiation moving forward.

Chapter 7

Avoiding Common Negotiating Pitfalls

Those with extensive experience at almost anything soon realize—and will often advise—that the best way to learn what to *do* in a particular situation is to consider what *not to do*. Want to live a healthy lifestyle? Here's what *not to do*—don't eat too many carbs and don't sit on the couch all day. It's a surprisingly simple formula for success in many aspects of life.

So it is for negotiating. Whether you're an experienced negotiator or are the new kid on the block, negotiating can be intimidating, confusing, and even frustrating. You are bound to make a few mistakes along the way. It's a natural part of the process of learning and perfecting your technique.

Even the most experienced negotiators learn from every negotiation. Like a game of chess, every negotiation unfolds differently, and there are lessons, nuances, and style points to be learned. You'll learn over time as you negotiate again and again, just as you honed your parenting techniques or leadership style after years of experience. Some of these corrections will happen "over-the-board" during every negotiation.

These fine-tuning efforts will happen naturally. That said, it's worth taking a few minutes to study and internalize some of the more common, and more serious, negotiating mistakes and pitfalls so that you can avoid them. Those mistakes and pitfalls are summarized in this chapter.

FAILING TO "SEE" THE WIN-WIN

The "Winner-Take-All" Trap

For many of us, nature often kicks in the drive to "win" as we approach most problems in life. We strive to come out on top, to come out ahead. At all costs, we want to avoid losing. These instincts are natural and healthy.

However, in combination with our egos, this natural tendency can transform us into ugly and determined monsters pretty quickly. When the ego gets involved, suddenly not only do we seek to win, but we also get an extra endorphin rush when the other party loses. We feel triumphant, like we've *really* done the job! It's true, as in many war games, that in some cases we can actually win more when the other party loses.

It might be a good way to fight a war, but a war is a conflict—and negotiating shouldn't be. Adopting too firm a "win" mentality causes us to fight too hard for the win, which makes enemies, escalations, and a bogged down negotiation. It also leads us to fail to "see" the win for the counterparty.

GETTING TO "YES," AVOIDING THE "NO"

As we reviewed previously, a negotiation goes faster and smoother—gets to "yes" more quickly—if the other side gets some wins, too. When each party walks away with some of their objectives, musts, and wants satisfied, the whole engagement goes more smoothly. Nobody walks away from the table with hard feelings, jobs lost, or other sources of pain. A relationship is sustained that will enable and encourage future negotiations. Long-term wins are better than short-term wins in this mindset.

So a winner-take-all mentality will bog down a negotiation or end it altogether. Don't go there! Don't go for the jugular and don't forget why you're there in the first place. "Win-win" is almost always better than "win."

"WINNER-TAKE-ALL" BLINDNESS

When you operate in a win-lose mentality, your ability to empathize with the other party becomes diminished. You simply revert to thinking about what *you* need, not what *they* need from the negotiation. When that happens, you set yourself up for failure, as the counterparty circles its wagons and goes on the defensive to protect their interests—they know you're not looking out for them.

Sometimes this leads the counterparty to turn the tables to play for a win at your expense. You didn't care about their goals, musts, or wants, so they don't care about yours. The resulting conflict is inevitable, and escalations of that conflict are likely.

The path to success is to get into their shoes, to understand their organization, key players, and objectives. Such empathy allows you to work out the *right* deal while not conceding or giving in too much. You make yourself sensitive to their needs and pressure points, and you try to accommodate as many as you can without compromising your own interests.

The bottom line is simple: If you try too hard to make them a "loser," you'll eventually lose as well.

DON'T FORGET NEGOTIATORS ARE PEOPLE, TOO

The Human Element

Another common negotiating mistake is to fail to understand and keep in sight the human aspects of a negotiation. Your counterparty is a person (or people), too; and while the goals, process, and facts of the negotiation should take priority, you mustn't forget the motives, emotions, nerves, efforts, personalities, organizational constraints, and other human factors of the negotiation.

If you take the human factors into account and deal with them effectively, rather than handling them as unpleasant surprises or distractions, you'll get to "yes" a lot sooner and with less friction and fewer hard feelings.

YES, SOME PEOPLE ARE DIFFICULT

People are individuals, and everyone has a different outlook on business and on life. Our own experiences influence how we see the rest of the world and react to what we encounter. When two or more parties sit down at the negotiating table, in person or virtually, each person has a different take on the engagement and operates from that viewpoint. This may lead to behaviors, many of which have been discussed in earlier chapters, that we may find difficult or even counterproductive to the negotiation.

The trick to dealing with such difficult players is to keep the focus on the subject matter and not on the individuals themselves.

Keep the end in mind and don't let these personalities exhaust you. Try not to walk on eggshells or worry about the other person; stay focused on the negotiation while trying within reason to meet the counterparty's tactical and emotional needs. Deal with this problem early on by reminding everyone of your common interests, goals, and objectives that brought you both to the table in the first place.

If They Seem to Have an Agenda

When you encounter negotiators who turn a negotiation from a fact-driven, structured process into a personal conflict or diatribe, you're probably dealing with individuals who have a personal agenda. That agenda can be simple—to come out on top or to "win." Or it can be more complex: to impress others at the table, including a boss, to deal with some other kind of organizational pressure, to get results or even a promotion, or to save a job.

Be the "White Hat" at the Table

If the personal agenda continues, take a moment to try to create a more comfortable atmosphere. Take a break if necessary; try to get the scoop in an informal conversation. If a manager is present, get her take if you can do that tactfully. Suggest that the personal issues and difficult behavior are getting in the way, that you've tried to accommodate, and that you should be afforded the same courtesy. Let the counterparty know that while you respect their situation and opinions, you'd rather focus on solutions that make the deal work, while not letting a personal agenda carry the day.

Be the "white hat" in the negotiation. Think positive, stay positive, and do what you can to neutralize the negative personal energy.

Generally it's worth taking the time to try to understand where the other party is coming from so that you can get the negotiation back on track. Is there a particular time, task pressure, or background you should know about? For the majority of personal issues, you're not likely to get a straight answer, but if you show some empathy and concern, it will help defuse the personal agenda.

It also helps to be open about where you stand and what your needs are. Don't place blame on the other party or get upset that everything seems so personal—that can make your opponent less likely to work through the problem with you. When you sense anger or aggression from another party, that emotion usually has nothing to do with you or the problem at hand; it's likely a reflection of something else in his personal or professional life. Getting it out in the open—or at least showing concern—can help both of you in your effort to arrive at a win-win conclusion.

Language Can Mean a Lot

The English language, as we all know, is highly nuanced. It contains many seemingly innocent words that can surprise you with how much power they hold. Tucked inside a harmless sentence, these words can create a tone that sounds offensive to anyone already on the defensive. Although you don't intend to hurt or cause pain, the counterparty misunderstands and reacts negatively.

The following word choices can help to avoid sounding too aggressive:

- *"I" versus "you."* Instead of saying, "You still didn't answer my question," rephrase the statement: "I'm sorry, I still don't understand. I think a few examples can give me a better idea." By placing the blame on yourself, you make it clear that you're not criticizing—and your counterparty will be more willing to communicate.

- *Negative versus positive.* Words such as "can't," "won't," "shouldn't," and "don't" should be used sparingly. Instead of saying, "I can't do that" try, "I have a few other options I'd like to get your opinion on." It might be easier to explain why you can't accept the offer if you present alternative solutions.

- *Watch the "buts."* Think of the word "but" as a cutoff point, a negative road sign, beyond which your counterpart may stop listening to what you're saying. He presents his idea, you rephrase it, and immediately you follow up with a "but" statement: "Our production costs are high, but the materials you're requesting are expensive." To the person on the defensive, this can sound like an attack on the original idea. It may feel to him as if it was wrong to have it in the first place. Try removing "but" from the sentence: "Production costs are high; the supplier charges X amount for these materials."

In all cases, you should be factual and use facts to back up your statements. Don't be, or appear to be, difficult.

DEALING WITH STONEWALLING

Sometimes a difficult person is one who uses a tough or challenging negotiating style. We've all seen it: A perfectly normal person with an otherwise accommodating or collaborative personality inexplicably becomes difficult to work with. This change may reflect a genuine difficulty in her life, or she may just be stonewalling.

There's a difference: Stonewalling is a ploy, like passive-aggressive behavior, and it is purposely used to draw your attention away from the subject you're discussing and/or to take control of the discussion in a quest to shift the balance of power. After several efforts to stonewall your proposals by asking irrelevant questions, changing the subject, or rejecting your offer outright, you might call her bluff by asking how serious she is about finishing the negotiation and getting to the win-win. Ask for a more detailed explanation of her opposition.

ALLOWING STRESS TO TAKE OVER

Make the Butterflies Fly in Formation

Think about the last time you were stressed out, particularly during or before a negotiation. You were sweating, heart pounding, and body on full alert. You had a headache, stomach ache, or nausea. For some of us, particularly less experienced negotiators, these reactions, or "pro-actions" as the case may be, are perfectly normal.

Many of us allow stress to take over. When the butterflies are flying, we have trouble thinking rationally or speaking clearly. We forget things. We screw up in the delivery. We may even look nervous or uncomfortable. These effects of stress can suggest weakness and be distracting to the flow of the negotiation.

The main antidote to stress—and public speakers will tell you this—is to use the nerves, the anxiety, the nervous energy itself, to get those butterflies to fly in formation. Don't be nervous, be assertive! The counterparty will never know that behind that self-assured front is a trembling, voice-cracking bundle of nerves. What they don't know, they don't know. Following are a few other tips for dealing with those butterflies.

THE BIG SECRET: PREPARATION

I can sum up the best antidote for stress and anxiety in one word: *preparation*. When you're prepared, you know what you're talking about, and when you know what you're talking about, you deliver it well. When you deliver it well, the anxiety goes away. This cycle of confidence does more to alleviate stress than any breathing exercise, handholding, medication, or any other tool or crutch possibly can.

We've already covered preparation (see Chapter 3), so there's no need to repeat it here. But just as real-estate agents talk about the "three Ls" most important in real estate, "location, location, and location," I submit that the "three Ps" of successful negotiation—and getting those butterflies to fly in formation—are "preparation, preparation, and preparation."

Always go there. You'll be glad you did, both for the negotiating outcome and for your own feelings and experience.

The "Scout's Motto" Works for Negotiating, Too

"Be prepared." That's what they teach young Boy and Girl Scouts, and you'd do well to take that lesson, too. Preparation is the antidote to stress, as it will give you the strength and confidence needed to navigate difficult waters. Preparation reduces anxiety before entering those waters, too. Both are vital to "keeping dry" in a negotiation.

Know What Sets You Off

Part of dealing proactively with stress is knowing and understanding your trigger points. Unforgiving negotiators can try to throw you off course by probing and exposing your weaknesses. They push your buttons. Your first line of defense against this tactic is to know your triggers, and to see them coming.

Here are a few common "hot buttons" to think about:

- Do you get defensive when your ideas are shot down?
- Do you easily take aggressive or defensive talk personally?
- Do you get insulted when someone doesn't agree with you?
- Are you easily offended or intimidated? How so?
- Are you too quick to give in or to please?

An aggressive negotiator will look for signs of these hot buttons and vulnerabilities. Recognition—and again, preparation—are the keys of your defense. Recognize when your counterparty is pushing your buttons, take a deep breath, and put on your professional face. Take a break if needed. If you are always prepared and stay prepared throughout the negotiation, then your ideas can't be legitimately shot down. You'll know and take comfort in that fact.

The main thing is to avoid letting stress get a foothold and take over your psyche.

Look Both Ways Before Crossing

This sound advice about crossing a road also applies to dealing with stress, particularly your counterparty's stress. Be sensitive to that stress; avoid traversing the other party's boundaries and building *their* stress levels. Think before reacting so as not to destroy the relationship by causing more stress. But don't surrender to stress either—either way you lose ground in the negotiation.

If you retaliate with anger, the counterparty may think he has you on his territory. You've been successfully put on the defensive, and everything goes downhill from there. Your measured, thoughtful responses will reduce stress—yours and theirs—and keep stress from building throughout the negotiation.

MISHANDLING CONCESSIONS

Giving Away Too Much or Too Little

Mismanaging concessions can cause you to give away the store if you give too many or give important ones up front. If too stingy with concessions, on the other hand, you may not get the concessions you seek, or may fail in the negotiation altogether. Here, we'll examine some specific mistakes that may cause your concessions to fall short of your goals.

THE DEAL IS IN THE DETAILS

When you sit down to prepare for the negotiation, you should not only "see" the deal but also "see" some of the details. This means doing some open-ended thinking about possible concessions. Write down the possibilities, large and small, that might be used at various points in the negotiation. Make sure you and your team are clear on which ones are the major pieces and which are the minor pawns in the game.

Evaluate the Competition!

With today's real-time access to information, it's easy to find and evaluate possible concessions. You have easy access to your own company's product offerings, shipping charges, and so forth, but you may be able to find out those of your competitors at the click of a mouse. Preparation includes evaluating the best set of concessions and the up-to-the-minute price, cost, and value of each. Chances are, your competition can arm you with all the information you need.

Don't Be Afraid to Ask

There's no need to feel greedy or afraid to ask for something you think the other party views as trivial. You never know what your counterpart will be willing to agree to. If you didn't ask for minor concessions you could have gotten, you'll probably regret it later. Aim high. Even if you think you're aiming too high, your goals might not seem to be as ambitious to your counterparty as they do to you.

GIVING UP TOO MUCH
(OR TOO LITTLE)

When it's your turn to make concessions, one of the most common mistakes is to think that the counterparty values what you're offering the same way you do. You'll inevitably under-concede or over-concede. Where you can, try to figure out how the concession fits into their business model. If they operate a "just in time" manufacturing line, you'll know immediately that in all likelihood expedited shipping is a concession of real value to them.

Again the best path is to prepare before the negotiation, and keep preparing during the negotiation by working to understand their business better during the conversation. You'll learn what makes them tick and what has the most (and least) value to them. That will help you make the right—and the fairest—offer.

Don't Forget to Ask for Something in Return

Remember—when making concessions, always ask for something in return. And remember, timing can be everything.

You might think it to be a good gesture to give away something because you figure you can ask for something in return later. Problem is, the later never really happens, or you feel compelled to give away something else when it comes. If you haven't been keeping track of concessions, you'll fail to see what you've given away and what you've received. You may also have to backtrack and re-evaluate the issues under discussion at the time you originally gave up the concession.

Get It in Writing

Always keep track of key points, decisions, and concessions in a negotiation. It will help you track what's happened, what's been given and received, and what further actions are necessary. Like a court record, written documentation provides a handy reference for everyone involved, and it makes drawing up an agreement a heck of a lot easier.

SOME FURTHER PITFALLS

Blowing the Close, Taking Wrong Risks, Loss of Focus

Because it involves creating and recording the final deal, blunders you make during the closing stage can be more costly than others already discussed. At closing, your negotiations are finalized; once the deal is done, there's no looking back. Here are some tips to consider to avoid these mistakes.

DON'T BE AFRAID TO BRING UP GREY AREAS OR MISTAKES

When re-examining the details of the negotiation, you might come across a miscalculation you made, an inaccuracy in your presentation, or an error in one of your concessions. You may even discover a concession that you didn't mean to make. When there's an error, bring it up immediately, even if it's embarrassing. The longer you wait, the more it becomes permanent. Worse, it may seem like you planted the error as part of a ploy.

Beyond having the courage to point out your own mistakes, have the courage to stand up to the other party's last-minute tactics. If the counterparty asks for an extra concession here and there, don't give in just to be the good guy and help close the deal faster. You may not be liked so much at this stage, but don't be afraid to say no.

Take Your Time

Making decisions because you feel pressured is one of the worst mistakes you can make, particularly during the closing. Take the time you need to finalize the agreements made—you'll be more confident about your decisions later. Some counterparties will try to pressure you deliberately, to get you to stop looking for concessions and make the deal. Bought a car lately?

While this slower pace may annoy your counterparty, don't be coerced into finalizing anything you're not ready for. Additionally, realize that most deadlines can be negotiated. Even if the extension is just for a few hours, use the extra time efficiently.

TAKING THE WRONG RISKS

The use of any negotiation strategy or tactic, whether used during the body of the negotiation or at closing, carries certain risks, and naturally, it's important to determine whether those risks are worth taking. Balance the risk, or the downside, of any negotiating point or concession, or even the time taken to pursue it, with the reward of that point or concession.

Many negotiators forget this and drive too hard on minutiae with little reward, or they do not drive hard enough on points that could prove very significant to the final outcome. If something's not worth haggling about, don't haggle about it! You'll waste time, credibility, and energy that can be used for more important and rewarding items.

A good rule of thumb for risk that works well, especially for investors, is this: Invest only what you can afford to lose. That model expands well beyond investing—any tactic or concession or offer should be measured against what you can afford to lose or give up in the negotiation. Keep in mind that what you lose can be short or long term, so don't forget about long-term consequences such as the opportunity to negotiate again.

Keep in mind that one of the biggest risks you can take is not preparing for the negotiation in the first place. Not only will a lack of preparation bog down the proceedings, you expose yourself to a multitude of unfavorable outcomes. Don't risk shortcutting this important step.

Don't Avoid Negotiating

Yes, negotiating can be stressful. But that doesn't suggest at all that you should avoid the negotiation. Sure, it would be nice to simply assume a deal or a key part of a deal and walk away. No risk, right? Not right.

You know what happens. When you assume a deal (or a point within a deal) is set, but neither you nor the counterparty have confirmed it, it usually goes wrong pretty quickly. Better to talk it out, even with a quick text, email, or phone call. Negotiations are part of an ongoing relationship (usually). Don't be an avoider. Avoidance behavior leads to mistakes short term and hurts the relationship long term.

Remember: while not negotiating seems to *avoid* risk, it actually *creates* it!

KEEP YOUR OBJECTIVES IN FOCUS

This mistake sails pretty close to the first pitfall, forgetting about the win-win. However, the mistake of losing focus is a little more general, covering goals and objectives subordinate to the overall win-win goal.

Losing focus on goals and objectives is a common—and dangerous—pitfall. You get so caught up in the moment or with the minutiae or personal dynamics of the situation that the original objectives fade into the background. The danger, of course, is that you don't accomplish what you set out to accomplish in the first place, or worse, you give away the store.

You really can't go wrong if you always keep a clear view of your main goals. If you and your team (and the other team) hew close to the original set of goals and objectives, then emotions like anger, anxiety, or the feeling of being overwhelmed won't distract you or throw the negotiation off track. Hopefully, you wrote down your objectives somewhere so you can keep track of them.

CASE STUDY

As president, CEO, and CVO of Filmographic Productions, you have been toiling away at the negotiating table for two hours. You've been showing your best video shorts, explaining your best production packages, and considering (but haven't yet offered) a few concessions, such as expedited production and turnaround at a reduced price.

Your clients, Dewey and Cheatum, both glaze over. You don't think you're connecting. In fact, the Dewey executives seem even a bit annoyed; they have work to do and they seem to want to get back to it.

What do you do? Have you inadvertently walked into a negotiating pitfall? It's time to take inventory.

Have you failed to see the win-win? Are you still on a win-win path? Have you thought through what will make them feel like a winner? You've come this far, and so far you've only presented your available schedule and price for filming their next commercial. Have you offered *anything* to make the deal more compelling and attractive to them? A price concession? An expedited timetable for production and delivery? Think about it. They didn't show up to the negotiation just to get your latest price quote.

Have you forgotten that Dewey and Cheatum are people, too? Are you taking too much of their time? Are you showing examples of real interest and relevance to them? Are you hogging the floor or doing something else to control the negotiation or to otherwise trigger an emotional response? Do the individuals at the table have personal agendas or issues that distract or detract from the negotiation?

What is their dynamic, anyway? Do they seem to be on the same page about what they want? Maybe you can help them get there.

THE IMPORTANCE OF STRESS

Is stress overly influencing the proceedings? Are you comfortable? Do they seem comfortable? Are you doing or saying anything to make them feel uncomfortable? Stop for a second to take inventory. Take a break if you need to, and ask them casually how business has been lately, how their last commercial worked out, how things are in their home life. Look for stress factors and try to soothe them.

Have you mishandled concessions anywhere along the way? Perhaps, as mentioned, you haven't made any yet; you've waited too long. Perhaps concessions you think you have made, like offering to meet on their premises, are irrelevant or even burdensome to them. Again, stop and take inventory. Have you tried to close the deal too soon, without giving the counterparty enough time on the floor?

Have you spent too much time discussing minutiae they consider unimportant or a waste of time? Again, remember that you are dealing with real people with real jobs and real time constraints. Make sure not to waste anyone's time in a negotiation, particularly with minutiae or by hogging the floor. Let them speak.

Remember that breaks can be used not just to rest and get coffee, but also to take inventory and to talk informally with your counterparties. If you feel antagonism or friction from one individual, try to talk with that individual. Find out if the irritant is related to process or product—that is, are they uncomfortable with the negotiation process and how it is unfolding, or are they uncomfortable with what you have to offer and the cost? A little informal research can yield some key insights, as well as soothe the nerves of both this individual and yourself. If you identify the pitfall properly and redirect the negotiation to address it, the response will feel positive when the negotiation reconvenes.

Outside of the necessary "bio break," there can be no better way to use breaks in a negotiation. Avoid pitfalls where you can, and fix them quickly and positively when they happen.

Chapter 8

High-Pressure Negotiating Tactics

As we've touched on in earlier chapters, negotiators can use numerous tactics and ploys to divert your attention away from the main facts and issues in a negotiation. Small tactical and emotional ploys can distract you, appeal to your emotions, or otherwise redirect the flow of exchange from task-oriented matters to more personal considerations. The usual antidote is to see these tactics coming and to calmly redirect the negotiation back to the objective high ground.

But there are several more outsized tactics and ploys to discuss, which I will refer to as high-pressure tactics, that are designed to force a counterparty to make hurried or seat-of-the-pants decisions out of fear of losing the deal altogether. These maneuvers can take the form of competitive offers, real and imaginary deadlines, and various kinds of ultimatums, all of which give the impression of leaving little room for further negotiation.

In today's fast-paced business world, the drive to reach a conclusion may seem more pressing than ever. Everything happens fast. Everyone goes fast in work, meetings, conversations—and negotiations. For this reason, it's important for you to discern true high-pressure tactics from those meant to simply cut to the chase and save time.

Once you learn how to recognize and counter these high-pressure tactics—which I will present in this chapter—you'll discover that you have more negotiating room than you think. You also may want to put a few of these tactics into play yourself.

THE UNREALISTIC FIRST OFFER

Exaggerating the Range of Give and Take

You walk into the negotiating venue. You take off your coat, exchange pleasantries, turn on your laptop, turn off your phone, sit down, and get down to business. Barely started, you blurt out the first offer: "We will sell you 1,000 widgets at $25," knowing full well you're prepared to deal them at $15 each.

Making an unrealistic first offer is one way to get a "feel" for how much (or how little) the counterparty is willing to take or to give you. You drop the offer on the table, then read the counterparty's response. First, based on their expression—anger, dissatisfaction, surprise, composure, or eagerness—you can get an idea about what is acceptable or within the scope of what they're willing to further negotiate. Second, the unrealistic first offer acts as a decoy, pulling the negotiation further toward the deal you're really willing to settle on.

Playing Defense

Of course, if you're on the receiving end of such an arm-twisting offer, your best defense is to be prepared. Know the market, and know what is in and out of bounds. Don't be afraid to display this knowledge to the counterparty. You'll gain their respect and head off their ability to use other such ploys. If you really aren't prepared and sense that an offer is unrealistic, hop online or even take a break to *get* informed quickly. Once you know that the offer is unrealistic, you can point that out, or counter with an unrealistic offer of your own.

Another way to play defense is to avoid getting an unrealistic offer altogether by being the one to make the first offer. This tactic also allows you to secure the starting point for the negotiation. Be careful not to put yourself at a disadvantage by making too generous an offer. Make it an informed—but slightly aggressive—offer. Remember that it's only a starting point.

Although it's a bit rude, you can counter the counterparty's unrealistic offer by ignoring it completely. Start talking about something else to tactfully deliver the message that you don't think the offer is worth considering.

Careful . . . Don't Offend the Counterparty

If you're using the unrealistic offer tactic, be careful. Your counterparty may take offense to this ploy, especially if they are well prepared and have researched the market to come up with their own number. If you sense that they're prepared, have extensive knowledge, and/or that they have several alternatives, don't start with a position that is too far off the mark. Their awareness of your intentions might make the whole tactic backfire. Never treat your counterparty as stupid or uninformed.

THE "ONE-TIME ONLY" OFFER

Act Now and You'll Get . . .

As a consumer, you get this one all the time. "Buy today, get 30 percent off." But *today*, and today only. What do you do? The impulse is to buy today—often whether you really need it or not—just to get the good deal. For if you wake up the next morning and decide "yes," then you will pay 30 percent more. And we can't let that happen, can we?

This rather typical retail ploy happens a lot in negotiations, too: "If you place the order today, we'll waive the shipping charge." Tempting, isn't it?

Recall the time and effort you put into preparing yourself for this negotiation. Do you want to let it all go out the window by letting this ploy sway you? A one-time offer ploy is designed to pressure you into closing the deal quickly. This pressure can get you off your pre-visualized path and can—though not always—lead to bad decisions. Sure, in today's fast-paced world, decisions can be and often need to be made quickly. But there's a difference between a fast decision and a hasty decision.

Playing Defense

Again, the best way to counter this ploy is to keep your cool and stay informed. Let your information and preparation guide you. Decide when you're ready to decide. Take your time, and make a little more time, by taking breaks or negotiating a little "bend" into the "firm" delivery date offer. Take the time (and ask for it if necessary) to do more research, ask questions, make sure the offer is consistent with your goals, and consult with your team.

As with the unrealistic offer, you can also ignore the tactic altogether. When the other party introduces the one-time only offer into the discussion, sidestep it (perhaps ignoring it altogether) by continuing to discuss ongoing issues or even bringing up some new ones. This passive-aggressive technique buys some time and likely attenuates your own emotional response. See if the one-time offer is brought to the table again before you respond. If it is, you'll be better prepared for it, and will be less likely to respond emotionally.

You can also counter with a one-time only offer of your own if you can put one together quickly enough. And remember, it's not a bad idea to prepare a few one-time onlys of your own ahead of time, not just for defense but to use this ploy to your team's advantage.

SCARCITY AND DELAY OF GAME

Act Now Before They're Gone . . .

Everyone has experienced this ploy in daily life. You go to the store to get a good sale price on an item, say a new high-definition TV. The salesperson calmly extolls the virtues of the TV—then calmly tells you that there are only two left, and when they're gone they're gone.

What do you do? Most likely, if you're pretty close to deciding this is the right deal anyhow, you buy the TV. Why? Because, as in the one-time offer ploy, you don't want to wake up the next morning thinking, "I could have gotten that great deal if only I had pulled the trigger."

Right. This happens all the time in negotiating. The counterparty might give you a false sense of scarcity of stock, production capacity, time, or some other factor that might sunder the deal if you don't take it *now*.

Playing Defense

When you suspect that the scarcity ploy is in play, the best approach is to ask questions to verify the scarcity. Try to determine if it is real: "Are there more of these TVs in the back? On order? Available online?" Also seek an alternative: "If I don't buy this TV today, what other televisions might offer nearly the same functionality at the same price?" You might find that there are plenty of alternatives and that a BATNA (Best Alternative to a Negotiated Agreement) will emerge—the scarcity of that model is real but not a big enough factor to get you to rush into a decision.

As with most ploys, the best defense is to see it coming, take the time to understand what's going on, ask questions, and make your decision calmly and professionally.

THE DELAY OF GAME

Delaying the game is the opposite of the "buy it today" deadline ploy. Delay tactics are used by negotiators in a variety of ways: to stall, to test your urgency, or to temporarily appease you.

When a counterparty stalls, she stops the negotiation, usually stating that your requests are "unacceptable," and that she needs more time to research, talk to the home office, and to respond. It can often appear as if she's digging in her heels to obstruct progress. She's using time as a defensive, and sometimes an offensive, weapon (she may be striving for you to make a concession to get things back on track).

Be aware that some stalling is probably legitimate; it may serve you well for her to contact her home office to get approval for a better offer. You'll have to judge on the spot whether the stall is being used as an aggressive tactic or a productive one.

More subtle is a delay purposely used to test your urgency. In such instances, the counterparty wants to read how desperate you are for the deal, for her business. Car salespeople do this, especially if they aren't too busy and have time to wait you out; they'll just step away for a bathroom break or cup of coffee, and then return to see how eager you are to make the deal.

Playing Defense

It's okay to give the other party some time to absorb everything so that she feels comfortable about the decisions she's about to make, but set a limit. When you suspect stalling, it's best to ask and find out what the obstructing element is, and then deal with it. Don't jump into making concessions just to grease the wheels of the negotiation. The delay/urgency test can seem like a silly cat-and-mouse game. Your best way to play it, though, is to see it coming, put on your poker face, and go on about your business in a professional manner.

Of course, one of the best ways to deal with this ploy is simply to whip out the committed-to agenda and remind everyone in the room what's supposed to happen and when.

Get Them to Say What They're Gonna Do

One of the best ways to defuse the delay-of-game bomb is to ask for specific time commitments for how long the counterparty will leave the negotiation. If the reason for the delay is real, she'll come back right away with something specific: "We need two hours to contact our production manager; we'll get back to you" or "I need to take a bio (bathroom) break; back in five." When she seems to struggle to come up with a specific answer, then it may be evidence that she's using a delay ploy.

FALSE BOTTOM LINES AND FALSE CONCESSIONS

Lines in the Sand That Blow Away

Here are two other negotiation ploys you see come up from time to time: the false bottom line and the false concession.

THE FALSE BOTTOM LINE PLOY

This one's common, too. If you are a parent, chances are you probably deploy it from time to time: the conveyance of a false or "absolute" bottom line beyond which you cannot go. "I can't buy you that $400 bicycle. You'll have to settle for the $350 one." Of course, you can spend $400 on a bike; you just choose not to.

In business, the false bottom lines are more subtle and tend to be driven more by external "reasons." For example, "I can't give you the $14 price on those widgets because my boss won't allow it; you'll have to take the $15 deal." Of course, at this point you never really know if the boss was even involved. The false or bogus bottom line acts as an ultimatum—a point beyond which the deal is not negotiable. It's a way to hasten the conclusion of the negotiation and to avoid further discussion that may lead to concessions.

Playing Defense

If you suspect a false bottom line, the first step is to probe its veracity; find out whether it's true or false. Ask what the limiting manager actually said, when, and why. Next, look at the deal as a "whole" deal and—if the price is firm at $15—ask if there are other concessions such as delivery, warranty, service and support, or other deliverables that can bring more value to your side of the table even if the price is firm. You may want to prepare a few concessions of your own. You'll get a better deal, and you might even get the price to move as the counterparty realizes that a price concession might be easier than some other concession.

Bottom line: when they throw a "bottom line" at you, the negotiation isn't over. In fact, it may have just begun.

THE FALSE CONCESSIONS PLOY

Suppose you walk into a store to look at the gorgeous jacket in the window. A salesperson approaches and says, "The jacket costs $75, but I'm having a good day; for you, I'll sell it for $65." She's letting you know up front that she's giving you the deal of the century. You smile politely and go back to the jacket to look it over. Suddenly she adds, "Okay, it seems you really like this jacket so I'll give it to you for $55."

Another discount? Now you're really on board! You inquire about the fiber content, wash instructions, and so on, and the salesperson reduces the price another $10. Feeling like you just hit the jackpot, you pay for the jacket and leave satisfied. Five minutes later another prospective customer walks in, starts looking at the jacket, wherein the keen salesperson says, "The jacket costs $85, but for you, I'll sell it for $75."

In both instances, the seller had a set figure in her mind all along. By exaggerating the price and then handing out a few concessions, she made it seem like a great bargain on the spot.

Playing Defense

This is not unlike the decoy tactic pointed out in Chapter 5. You've been given a figure that artificially assigns a higher value to the item. When the counterparty improves upon that figure, you feel as if you've gotten a better deal. Your emotions take over and you snap it up, not realizing that you've been played to get you to think the deal is better than it is.

The best defense, aside from preparation—say, some research into what those jackets cost in other stores—is to somehow validate the original price. Look for a price tag, a price list, perhaps evidence of past sales. Think of the original price in a vacuum (that is, without the discounts). Is it anything close to realistic for that item? Finally, ask why the salesperson is giving such aggressive discounts. "Having a good day" or "It's sunny outside" probably aren't good enough reasons. Also, in a more complex deal, there's a good chance that if you aren't being asked for any concessions of your own, then the ones you're being given may not be real. Once you figure out what's real and what's false, act rationally; don't let your emotions decide.

COMPETITION AND DEADLINES

Gaining Leverage with External Pressure

Two more ploys involve putting pressure on a negotiation in order to force concessions and/or hasty decisions that may lead to bad or unexpected results.

THE COMPETITION PLOY

Here, real competition or competitive offerings are used as a type of shill in the negotiation. This tactic works, for example, when trying to choose a cell phone carrier. You might visit several wireless providers to hear their offers. When you find one that seems to suit you best, mention that you also looked into Company B and were quoted a rate that you're seriously considering. Nine times out of ten, you'll get another offer right away. Simply continue this approach until the best deal presents itself.

Playing Defense

Suppose the roles reverse; your counterparty is presenting several competitive options to get a better deal out of you. You feel the pressure. However, you may or may not know what the competitors actually offer (if you're prepared, you *will* know!). If you're not completely up to speed on the competitors, ask for some details on the other offers. Find out if there's a "value proposition" where some other feature, such as data service or reception coverage, is diminished in order to produce the good price. If the counterparty doesn't know, he may have been bluffing all along; if he *does* know, you'll learn a lot more about the competition. If you determine that the competitive offers are real and valid, negotiate accordingly; if you find out they're not, well, negotiate accordingly.

THE DEADLINE PLOY

Deadlines—either intermediate or final—can be used not only to keep a negotiation on track but also to put pressure on negotiators. Especially with today's fast-paced negotiations, deadlines may be in a day, in a few hours, or even in a few minutes—there's almost always a deadline somewhere.

As a high-pressure tactic, deadlines, especially if not mutually agreed on beforehand, are often used to ask for last-minute concessions. People are naturally more willing to compromise when facing time restraints. When too much is coming at us all at once, it's easier to get rid of the most immediate and stressing factor(s) than to take the time to work them out. Have a labor contract expiring next Monday? You'd better be prepared to make some concessions to get the revision done.

Playing Defense

Naturally, the first line of defense against this ploy is to make sure the deadline is real. Deadlines, especially unilateral deadlines set by one party, may be real or may be arbitrary as part of a tactic to push a deal. Probe the origin and reason for the deadline by asking questions. Ask for flexibility in the deadline also; rarely are time-based reasons absolute. The answers can give you an idea whether the deadline is real and can also indicate whether the deadline itself is a negotiating point.

Some deadlines may be more informal or made out of convenience than others. "I have to catch a flight at three o'clock this afternoon" indicates a deadline, but perhaps not an insurmountable one as a later flight may be available or the discussion can continue online. Again, a few questions—and a willingness to offer a concession to entice the counterparty to stay longer—might help.

LAST-MINUTE OFFERS AND WITHHOLDING INFORMATION

Two Final Pressure Ploys to Influence an Outcome

As I've described, the purpose of pressure tactics is often to throw you off balance so you make mistakes and give away more than you intended. These last two tactics are both designed to do that.

THE LAST-MINUTE OFFERS PLOY

Just about when you're ready to close your laptop and close the deal, you hear, "Wait! We've got another counteroffer for you!" Of course, what is your frame of mind at that point? You're done—that's what.

When you're finished or close to finished with anything—say, that college term paper or final exams—the last thing you want to do is to revisit it all. You'd be willing to give something, anything, not to have to revise that term paper. So what are you likely to do? Concede something, just to *keep* it done. That, of course, is what your counterparty seeks. Similarly, your landlord might hold off on telling you about a rent increase until the very end of the month because by then, you're already in the mindset that you're staying for another month, not to mention that it would be hard to move on such short notice anyway.

Playing Defense

This ploy is hard to defend against, because you don't know what may be coming at the last minute. If your counterparty has done this before, of course, you can say something about it as you lay out the "ground rules" for this latest negotiation. You can also ask for an extended deadline. This delay gives you time to regroup and get back into the negotiating frame of mind: You want to prevent yourself from acting too hastily in an emotional attempt not to scotch a done deal.

Reaching Quick Settlements

Tight deadlines can lead to quick settlements, and the team with the most effective "quick settlement" approach can come out ahead. Effective quick settlements happen when one or both teams are informed and organized, allowing for fast and effective presentation. Quick settlements can bring relief to both sides when tight deadlines are involved, and are likely to lead to a greater win for the side that leads in making the settlement. But if you're being subjected to a quick settlement, make sure the balance of power is relatively equal and that you have time to consider and prepare a response.

Particularly in today's fast-paced negotiating era, the ability to make, and respond to, a quick settlement is an important asset in your negotiation toolkit.

THE WITHHOLDING INFORMATION PLOY

Somewhat similar to the last-minute offer, a counterparty may wait until the deadline is near to disclose additional information, leaving you little time to digest the new details. He wants to see if you'll give in without fully absorbing the new information completely. "Well now, if you're interested in some of these widgets in white, I currently have a surplus of that color; I can give them to you for $13," might be an example of such a ploy if you were about to take the deal at $15. Now you must decide quickly if white is okay ... including trying to discern if he was really trying to get rid of the white ones all along for some reason.

Playing Defense

The defense is simple: Ask for more time. Keep your balance; judge objectively. In order to restore equilibrium, you may also take some of your concessions off the table or disclose some new information of your own for the counterparty to consider.

Wanting It Now: The Use of Deadlines As a Ploy

Most concessions are made toward the end of a negotiation's deadline, if there is one. The explanation is simple. The more time the two parties invest in the negotiation process, the less likely they will be to backtrack or pull out. If one party demands new concessions, the counterparty is more likely to give in to bring the negotiations to a successful end. However, sitting tight until the end and deploying deadline tricks such as disclosing new information is a high-risk strategy; you'll need patience and self-confidence to do it.

Your counterparty is aware of deadline pressures and tricks to exploit them, too. Realize this, and don't be afraid to manage the deadlines themselves by extending them or tightening them as necessary to keep control of the agenda. Know the deadlines and use them to maintain the balance of power in the negotiation.

When the eleventh hour rolls around, don't be opposed to extending the negotiation if it means you can work out the best deal with more time. The best win-win may come this way.

CASE STUDY

Does the Competitor Have a Longer Lens?

Despite your offer to do an expedited production for free, Dewey and Cheatum continue to drag their feet; the negotiating session drags on. It seems that every time you try to settle a point, the Dewey executives want to move to something else. Right now they're focused on your competition.

As the president/CEO/CVO of Filmographic Productions, you're hearing: "Yes, that's a nice offer, but your competition CMY Video offers us Services X and Y for $Z less than you do."

Now, is it for real, or is Dewey using it as a negotiation ploy? You'd jump out of your skin to know.

The first thing to do (that is, if you haven't prepped yourself with your competition's offerings already by looking at their sites and in particular talking to some of their clients) is to go online. Ask for a break if necessary. See if CMY even does the kind of work you're doing. When you've done your research, one of your first replies might be, "You know, CMY Video mainly does educational videos. These have a completely different look and production quality. I'm not even sure they've ever filmed a TV commercial."

In this case you've defused the ploy by knowing the competition. It's even better if you know that they haven't filmed *any* commercials—the less ambiguity the better.

You might remind Dewey and Cheatum that CMY is a big national chain and that they have to fly a crew out from New York. As such, they would be less flexible; what if it happened to be raining the day they came to film your outdoor commercial? What if they have retakes that can't be done because of flight scheduling?

Negotiating under high-pressure ploys often means taking what's thrown at you, and throwing it back with something better, or with something your client never thought of.

All done, of course in a professional and courteous manner.

Chapter 9

When to Close, How to Close, and When to Walk Away

This analogy may be a little worn, but the phases of the negotiation process resemble a dating relationship. There's a period of initial discovery, a typically longer and more stable period of give-and-take, followed by a conclusion and resolution to move forward . . . or not. Like a dating sequence, as you and your counterparty move forward, with or without a deadline you'll eventually want to finalize the deal.

The deal may come straight out of a period of harmonious discussion, or it might be forced by a deadline. Or it may be the product of mutual agreement after a long period of negotiation. You might be close to a deal with simply a few details to work out, or you might be miles apart and not ready to "tie the knot" just yet. This chapter is about preparing for these late resolution stages of the negotiating process, including finding late win-wins, resolving deadlocks and last-minute objections, making last-minute changes, and preparing the final agreement.

SOLVING UNEQUAL BARGAINING PROBLEMS

Dealing with One-Sided Deals

If the negotiation has been smooth up to this point, the terms and concessions should be fairly easy to document and to spin up into a deal. If there's time, and if good notes have been taken as you go, the negotiating team "scribe" can document all elements of the deal on the spot, draw up the final agreement, and get the necessary approvals or signatures, real or virtual, on the spot.

Formulating the agreement can be formal, or it can be a matter of taking notes and distributing them to the parties later for final review and ratification. Sometimes it helps to give the deal some time to sit and gel in everyone's mind before finalizing it—perhaps in a subsequent meeting or conference. If you feel the deal is a bit biased in your favor, you may want to avoid this "cooling off" period and proceed with the final deal immediately.

If the deal negotiated so far stops short of win-win, there may be more work to do. It's usually okay to come out a little ahead, but when the deal seems too one-sided, problems will creep in, ranging from immediate (dis)approval from superiors, advisors, or legal teams to damaging the long-term relationship between you and the counterparty. You can employ various tactics to resolve one-sided deals, and if they can't be resolved, setting the negotiation aside for now may be the best option.

FIXING THE WIN-LOSE OUTCOME

Win-lose deals come about when strong positional negotiating tactics are used, often marked by emotional ploys, aggressive behaviors, poor preparation, and/or tight deadlines. Win-lose deals happen when counterparties dig in too deeply and fail to work toward the win-win. Such stubbornness and reluctance to "lose" comes about out of short-sightedness and, in many cases, ego. The negotiation has become as much about personal gain as it has about business or objective gain. Goals and objectives on one or both sides won't be met.

The best way to deal with this situation is to stop. Pause the negotiation and exercise some leadership, reaffirm the win-win goal, and take inventory of what each side has won and lost. Remind everyone at the table that short-term and long-term success is couched in a win-win deal. The size of the wins doesn't have to be equal, but both sides should achieve something toward their goals.

You might back up to an agreed-upon point in the discussion and start there, moving forward with a more equal division of concessions. In a particularly difficult negotiation, time permitting, you might stop for the day and give each side some time to revisualize the deal that would work best for all.

DEADLOCK: WHEN NOBODY WINS

A deadlock occurs when negotiations come to an impasse. Both parties have dug in on a point and/or have used up all their concessions. Progress seems out of reach; no matter how many reviews or revisits of the issues, favorable resolutions are nowhere in sight. At the moment, both parties lose because neither accomplished their goals. Furthermore, the emotional response to such a stalemate can be anger and blame, and potentially a communication collapse. Both parties withdraw from the discussion and perhaps, wanting to save face and not budge, they refuse to go back and break off the talks. Result: a lose-lose scenario.

Deadlock often occurs because the best possible solution hasn't yet been discovered. If one or both counterparties seem inflexible, something important may be missing from the discussion, something that could resolve the conflict. There may be an 800-pound-gorilla issue in the room that nobody has brought up—for instance, background financial problems in a business negotiation or emotional problems when negotiating with your teenager. Or the problem may be a smaller tactical issue like delivery time or gas money that hasn't been discussed but would surely grease the wheels toward getting to where you'd both like to go.

As in most productive communication, it pays to be sensitive, positive, and to ask questions and listen in a positive way. Again, you or another member of either of the negotiating teams should step back, take inventory of the current deal, and progress toward that deal: where you are and how you got there. By reviewing the steps, you might discover where it went awry, and where one or both teams might be able to interject something. That something might be a bit of information, a new concession, or an idea. Regardless, the objective is to find a way to once again move things forward.

A break will help you gather and collect your thoughts before you do this. Another tactic is to bring someone into the review who hasn't witnessed or been active in the negotiation so far. That individual may be able to spot potential resolution points and suggest ways to move forward. Someone at the table who hasn't been too active in the negotiation thus far can also serve this purpose.

It never hurts to review the objectives of the negotiation. Sometimes it's better to focus on what you have accomplished than what you haven't. Such a review gets the positive energy back into the room and helps both parties realize they can agree on something.

Be the One, Not the Ten

I call it the "one in ten" syndrome, and it happens a lot in business. For every one individual moving things forward with positive energy, there are nine other people questioning tactics, finding faults and errors, even nitpicking the PowerPoint presentation. It's a truth in human nature and especially of bureaucracies that it's easier to find fault with someone else's work than to do constructive work of our own.

It happens all the time in negotiations. Everyone in the room becomes a critic and pipes in with what's wrong with a particular element of a deal. In their mind, they're participating, contributing, and showing everyone how smart they are. In reality, they're just bringing negative energy to the table.

Negative energy will almost always slow or derail any business meeting, including a negotiation. When team members get fixated on finding fault, it becomes a vicious cycle; *everyone* starts doing it. It is very difficult to move forward. As a leader, or a leading team member, try to redirect this energy toward the positive. When someone chimes in with a negative or a "fault," give them the floor and ask them to come up with a solution that would make that element *not* faulty; a solution that would breathe life into the deal.

Focus on the positive and nitpick the nitpickers, and you'll return the negotiation to a "fast, friendly, and effective" format.

KNOWING WHEN TO OPT OUT

Sometimes, no matter how much time you've invested into making a deal work, you reach a point where it feels like it's time to walk away. The reasons might be readily apparent—you're not satisfied with the final offer, you have new information, you're uncomfortable with the other party and their tactics, one (or more) alternative deals seem better, or you want to research a better alternative.

The reasons could be more subtle, psychological, or intuitive. For example, if your counterparty has been difficult to work with or untrustworthy from the beginning, you'll wonder about dealing with this person or organization through the life of the contract; his behavior may not improve. You may also not want to negotiate with him again.

Opting out can be as much a matter of instinct as it is of facts or concrete evidence. When it feels like the counterparty is being especially difficult or is not seeking the win-win, withdrawing from the negotiation not only saves time, stress, and sometimes money, but it also sends a message: You're too far apart, factually or emotionally, to continue. Most likely, if there is a win-win somewhere in sight, the counterparty will come back to the table. If the counterparty doesn't come back, you may assume that it wouldn't have worked anyway. It's time to move forward to negotiate with someone else.

There's No "I" in "TEAM"

The opt-out decision is usually instinctive; however, if you're negotiating as part of a team, make the decision as a team. If you are acting out of emotion, other team members can set you straight or even help find a solution. Don't opt out before other alternatives are exhausted.

FINALIZING THE DEAL

The End Is in Sight!

Okay, here's another scenario: The negotiation has worked and you're almost there! Exciting as that may sound, there are still a few more challenges to overcome. Some of these challenges may test you but will also avoid roadblocks to reaching a well-deserved closure.

The first step is to review—to take inventory—of where you are so far. Clarify or "add color" (that is, detail) to points that need more detail or clarity (next day delivery—is that morning or afternoon?). When you're in the thick of a negotiation, it's easy to get caught up swapping concessions and making offers and counteroffers. You're concerned about everything from the details of what you're getting and giving to deciphering the other person's body language, mood, and sincerity all at once. Step back, taking a break if necessary, to review all points of the negotiation against your list of goals, musts, and wants.

A lot will happen during the final stages of the negotiation. Here are a few more helpful tips.

Beware the Last-Minute Bargain

I mentioned this in earlier chapters but it bears repeating: People have a natural tendency to panic when time is almost up. They fear leaving something out or not achieving goals, or even losing the deal altogether. As a result, amendments to the deal from both sides can come out of the woodwork at closing time. Watch closely to make sure they don't materially alter the deal, and above all, don't give away the store just to get the deal done.

SEPARATE CLOSURE FROM THE REST

When the time seems right, and you're ready to close, ask your counterparty if she agrees that it's time. If so, clearly state that everything discussed from here on out will be part of the closure. The closure may be scheduled into the agenda already but it usually doesn't hurt to do it sooner if you're ready. More often the initiation of closure is simply agreed to along the way. If your counterparty isn't quite ready, agree to more time if requested.

Separating the closure from the rest of the negotiation does two things. First, it puts both parties in a closing frame of mind, toward documenting and fine-tuning *what already has been* discussed as opposed to introducing new items into the negotiation. Second, and related, a separated closure makes it less likely that something new will be added to complicate the negotiation or tip it into one party's favor. It also brings something of a fresh beginning if both parties are worn out from the effort put in thus far.

Working Through Objections

Although the closure received a go-ahead from both parties, problems could arise if one party objects to one or more of the terms being reviewed. If this happens, you'll have to use your best negotiating skills, and a degree of patience, to work through the objections and preclude a deadlock. If there's a disagreement, it's best to validate it; that way your counterpart will be more likely to treat you with the same courtesy. Then work with—not against—the counterparty to resolve the disagreement.

Deal with issues and objections quickly. It becomes harder once you're close to closing an agreement.

Bring Out the Objection Underneath

If you sense there's a deeper issue than your counterparty is stating, ask some exploratory questions to coax it out. You might say something like, "It seems like something about this topic isn't quite right. Is there another issue that concerns you?"

Be empathetic and offer to help. Remember, it's all about finding the win-win.

THE CLOSE: WHEN AND HOW

When it comes time to close, there are some obvious and some not-so-obvious signals that the moment is right to make the move. If it seems that most goals and objectives of both counterparties have been achieved, then it might be time to move forward into the close.

A first step for both parties is to review notes made throughout the course of the discussion. In a slower, deeper negotiation this is important because you may not remember every detail, or you may remember *too many* details and lose the strategic forest among the tactical trees. (What did you really agree on?) Likewise, reviewing notes is important in a fast-paced negotiation because everything happens so fast.

It often helps to outline all the agreements made, and the details and terms that were discussed, on a separate sheet of paper or electronic document. List the terms of the deal, including concessions, and any contingencies or items that require further detail or research. Write everything down as clearly as you understand it. If all goes well, these documents will become the terms of your agreement.

Next, compare your notes with those of your counterparty, or if he didn't take notes, read each item on your list out loud. The point is to have both of you not just hear but *understand* the agreement in the same way. If you thought your counterparty was paying the shipping charges in exchange for a 20 percent discount on production fees but he thought he was paying 20 percent of the shipping, then you'll need to work that out.

When Is the Deal a Deal?

From a legal standpoint, closure occurs when all the agreed-upon terms are finalized into a clear, binding, signed contract, witnessed and verified by all parties. Read the entire agreement, and sign only when you're ready. The less you can leave open to interpretation, the better.

Last-Minute Concessions

When the close isn't going as smoothly as hoped, and the other party is still unable to accept the conditions as they stand, you might want to offer a last-minute concession to push the deal into completion. Not a big one that changes the whole deal—but one that is worth something to them. This gesture shows a willingness to sacrifice something to make the deal work for both of you. Getting things done now may well be worth more than the value of the minor concession.

Again, don't make this last-minute concession a centerpiece of the negotiation.

What's Stopping You?

As strange as it may sound, some people never really seem to *want* to reach the end of a negotiation. There may be some anxiety in a closing that was not present during the mainstream negotiation. The deal might represent a big step and a big commitment both for the counterparty's business and for their professional careers.

Remember that feeling you had when you bought your first car? First computer? First home? After spending months researching, comparing, and reworking your budget to make the best choice, you came to the end of the negotiation pensive, ecstatic, and unsure all at once. Likewise, your counterparty might be concerned that not all bases have been covered and facts understood. This especially might be the case in a rapid-fire negotiation. So how do you make it through the close? You can:

- Overcome fear by preparation; if still worried, take time out to prepare more.
- Control doubts about details by writing down the details and reviewing them.
- Don't drag your feet. You may lose your counterparty's respect and possibly the deal.

All these tips depend on having faith in yourself, which in turn depends on your level of preparation both before and during the negotiation.

Pat the Team on the Back

A little enthusiasm goes a long way, especially when the counterparty hesitates. A few encouraging words may help remind everyone about the objectives they accomplished and what the deal means to both sides of the table. Sometimes hearing the list of accomplishments out loud makes a bigger impact than just quietly thinking them over. If you're delivering the review, remind everyone how they benefit from each element of the agreement.

Positive energy and the energy engendered by accomplishment are contagious and go a long way toward sealing the deal and building an effective long-term relationship.

Rewards Never Hurt

Matters in both your business and personal life can seem to go just a little bit better if there's some kind of reward in sight. Not just a completed job or deal or household budget, but a true reward. I've found that families and family members make budgets and adhere to budgets better if there's some kind of perk at the end of the exercise: a nice dinner, some entertainment, a promise to take a small vacation, or some such thing.

The same can hold true for a business negotiation. If everyone reaches an agreed win-win prior to the deadline, why not indulge in a nice dinner or give everyone on the team a gift card or a free sample of your merchandise? The promise of such a reward can be made in advance or on the fly.

Of course, don't make the reward too big, since it might throw the negotiation for the sake of receiving the reward. Common sense, as always, should prevail.

START WITH THE END IN MIND—FOR THE CLOSE, TOO

Visualize the *Final* Deal

Just as "seeing the deal" is key to a successful preparation for the negotiation, "seeing" the close also helps, not only with the close itself but with the entire negotiation. Indeed, seeing the close is an important part of seeing the deal.

All the steps of the negotiation process—research, planning, bargaining, relationship building—should be undertaken with the eventual close in mind. When researching and preparing, consider terms or concessions you might ask for at the last minute to seal the deal. Think about what questions or objections your counterparty may have, and come up with answers in advance. Consider what might cause an impasse, and what you might do to avoid it.

Throughout the negotiation, exercise the right amount of leadership to create a positive environment and energy to support an effective close. You want to satisfy your goals and get the deal that makes the satisfaction of those goals official. You also want to lay the groundwork for the next negotiation.

Am I Leading? Negotiating? Or Both?

This isn't a leadership book. Or is it?

Actually, I believe it is. Allow me to explain.

First off, I'd like to give you my definition of leadership I developed while examining Steve Jobs's leadership style for my book *What Would Steve Jobs Do?* (McGraw-Hill, 2012):

"Leadership is getting people to *want to*—and to *be able to*—do something important."

Say you're a member of a two-sided team attempting to accomplish something important (if it wasn't important, you probably wouldn't be negotiating, right?). As a good party to the negotiation, you want to get to the end you had in mind, and so why not help create an environment where the negotiators *want to* find the win-win and are *able to* do so?

When you exercise such leadership by being positive, removing barriers, suggesting improvements, dealing with emotions, and making people feel at ease, among many other tools of leadership, you not only foster the negotiation but also enhance your reputation among your peers (and managers, too).

In every way, being a leader in a negotiation reflects well on you as a professional. Seize the opportunity!

DON'T RUSH THE CLOSE

Remember, closing is a separate step that requires as much diligence as the other steps. You should never rush through it. Here are the closing checkpoints you should be sure you follow through on:

1. First, confirm that everyone is in agreement that it's time to close. If there are still large disagreements, open issues, or items of research to be done, it probably isn't time to close.
2. Review the agenda to be sure everything has been covered.
3. Review your notes, including agreements and concessions, to verify coverage and completion of all terms and conditions.

4. Create to-do lists, if needed, for items to follow up on. Delegate those items to team members and provide clear deadlines for follow-up.

5. Make a clear transition to the close. Tell the team that's where they are and set a mini-agenda for the close itself: what items still need to be discussed and where and how the final agreement will emerge.

A separate, well-defined close session with a clear timetable and precise actions will help you get through this important stage and achieve the overall deal. By now, if all has gone well, you and your counterparty are acting as a single team looking to get the win-win deal done together.

Integrity, Always

Beyond leadership, another vital key to fast, friendly, and effective negotiating is *integrity*—the ability to make a commitment and to follow through on the promises you make. In the interest of this, it is very important that you understand all of the terms you're agreeing to. Don't kick the can down the road by making sloppy agreements. It will come back to haunt you later; your next negotiation could turn out to be a nightmare! As well, you'll have to live with a bad deal between now and then.

CASE STUDY

Closing the Deal

The coffee pot is cold, the plate of Danish pastries is empty, and the energy level in the room is winding down, though it's still positive. You've made a strong case for your company, Filmographic Productions, and Dewey and Cheatum have agreed to most of your points. There are a few details to still work out, but your sense is that further discussion might needlessly annoy people and conceivably reintroduce issues that have already been settled.

So you take a deep breath and say, "I think we're at the point of wrapping this up. Can I just run down a brief list of what we've agreed to and what we're still discussing? Then I believe we could leave these smaller points to the lawyers to work out."

The whole process has been building toward this moment: coming to agreement and doing the deal. You've seen the deal all along; now you're close to getting it done and getting it in writing. So you take charge. You offer to help wind up the negotiation and to lead the close. You announce your willingness to lead the close—assuming everyone else at the table is ready. A few yesses and nods indicate that it is so; it's time to close the negotiation and the deal.

You take a break to create a short, back-of-napkin agenda for the close. You will share that agenda, including the items to review or cover at the close. You also set an amount of time, say, one hour, that you think it will take to work the close.

During the close you cover the following:

1. You review the best set of notes available with the teams (combining the notes of multiple team members if necessary). As

you walk through the notes, you acknowledge what's been accomplished and give recognition to what concessions or contributions have been made: "Mr. Dewey made a very good point about this issue, so we agreed . . ."

2. With team input, you establish clear agreement on which points haven't yet been settled and set a time frame for working them out: "We can ask our lawyers to meet on these points next week and have a formalized agreement by May 30. Does that sound okay?"

3. You lay out a schedule to write the contract and offer to have your team do it if appropriate. This will give you more control over the precise wording of the terms of the agreement and places the initiative firmly with you.

4. You reward the effort. As everyone stands up, you say, cheerfully, "I think this calls for a celebration. How about if Filmographic treats us all to a drink at the restaurant next door to celebrate our new working relationship?"

It's amazing, when it all goes well, how the "divide" between the two counterparties melts away and you all begin to function as one happy team. It's a great feeling, and one that bodes well for the future.

Chapter 10

Finalizing the Agreement

You've worked hard. You've found the win-win that gives both parties a sense of success. You've outlined the terms of the deal; who does what, where, when, and how. Both parties have agreed to the deal at a high level and at a level of detail sufficient to proceed.

Now what? You need to document the deal. You need to get it in writing, first, so everyone knows the terms and what to do to meet them; and second, so that you have something to refer back to in case anything isn't clear or gets lost in the fog of time. Just as important for most deals (perhaps excluding deals with your teenage son) is that you document them so as to make them legally binding. Legal documents make sure that expectations are clear and that remedies are available in case certain terms aren't adhered to.

This is already starting to sound like "legalese" language, and that is, in part, my intent. This chapter is about formalizing your deal into an agreement, and where necessary, a formal, written, and legally binding contract. I can't include an entire course in business law in a single chapter, nor can I provide you with legal counsel in this book. However, I can give you some basics to be aware of as you proceed and as you seek the advice of specialists in creating and enforcing the deal.

ELEMENTS OF AN AGREEMENT

Getting to a Contract

I will use the words *agreement* and *contract* somewhat interchangeably here; the basics are the same except that a contract is more formal and is typically written using a boilerplate form with all the appropriate legal language and disclosure. Assuming that you're not a practicing attorney, your job as a negotiator is typically to develop the agreement. You should then let the lawyers and/or contract specialists massage the details, finalize the language, and prepare the final document(s).

Your job is to negotiate the deal and come up with a mutually satisfactory agreement, then to evolve that agreement into a binding contract typically with the help of specialists. The process is straightforward:

DEAL → AGREEMENT → CONTRACT

Although the details of an agreement are normally not fleshed out until the end of a negotiation, it's important to keep them in mind throughout the entire negotiation process. It is important to keep track not only of the major terms but also the nuances and possible remedies if terms aren't or can't be adhered to. Remedies can be a substitute good or service, or can simply be a renegotiation of that point. Throughout the negotiation, good note taking will not only ensure that you include everything you want in the contract, but it will also help clear up any fuzzy points discussed informally or beforehand.

SIMPLE OR COMPLEX?

While I just made contracts sound elaborate and precise down to the *nth* detail, they can also be a simple one- or two-line memo or statement of what someone intends to do in exchange for what. Don't get caught up in trying to make them too complex and wordy—your goal is to document the deal so that:

1. Both parties can perform with little ambiguity
2. Both parties know what constitutes nonperformance
3. Both parties, where necessary, know the remedies if one side doesn't perform

The contract should be concise and should cover the main points of the deal, no more, no less.

TYPES OF CONTRACTS

Contracts serve to record agreements that two or more parties have made with each other and to outline the terms of those agreements. A good contract protects the promises, expectations, and investments of the parties involved, and if done right, is sufficient to be enforced such that disputes can be resolved in a court of law.

Contracts can range from a simple template form (perhaps downloaded from an online source) to specific custom-written documents that are tailored to the specific deal.

Form Contracts

Form or boilerplate contracts are precrafted templates used for basic, oft-repeated agreements. Most real estate agencies and mortgage brokers will use the same form contract for every client. These boilerplates list the conditions, limitations, and delivery expectations agreed to, and they are amended only to reflect the terms and provisions unique to each situation. The set-in-stone appearance of this type of contract may seem intimidating, but you can change the form, to add or delete items as needed, so long as both parties agree and accept the changes (usually by initialing the change).

THE THREE MAIN PARTS OF A CONTRACT

Offer, Consideration, Acceptance

At its roots, a contract has three major and clearly identifiable parts: the *offer*, the *consideration*, and the *acceptance*.

The offer is straightforward: "We at Company A will produce and deliver 1,000 widgets per month for the next six months." The consideration is the payment: "Company B will pay $25 per widget, with a discount of 1 percent if paid within thirty days." The acceptance is the signed return of that agreement with any other agreed-to terms that come in along the way.

Discussions Outside the Negotiation

Discussions outside the negotiation can affect the deal, too. Don't forget to jot down notes after each phone call, email, and other communication. Also mark the date and time the contact took place so any changes that were discussed are on record. Make sure to amend the agreement notes with the results of these discussions to get them into the record.

As we'll see shortly, verbal (and "e") contracts are usually considered binding.

Of course, the offer and consideration can come in many forms—but a contract without a clear offer, clear consideration, or a clear acceptance isn't a contract. Period.

DRAFTING AGREEMENTS AND CONTRACTS

As the negotiation winds down, the next decision is who will draft the agreement. Then you need to decide who will take responsibility for finalizing the contract. Make sure everyone agrees on who leads these tasks.

Why Volunteer to Write the Agreement?

In his book, *The Negotiation Toolkit: How to Get Exactly What You Want in Any Business or Personal Situation*, Roger J. Volkema suggests that offering to write up the agreement benefits you in two ways. First, it relieves the other party of the task and can be viewed as gracious and generous. Second—and more important—writing the agreement gives you some control over what it says and how it says it.

The first step in drafting an agreement is to summarize the notes, be it a single set of notes taken by a single scribe or negotiation leader or a composite of several sets of notes. If the notes aren't sufficient, you may have to go back to revisit certain negotiation points; take the time to do so. Otherwise you risk having crucial details left out, muddled, misconstrued, or denied. Notes should include, or reference, the specific terms and benefits for both you and the counterparty, including deliverables, consideration, and timing, including:

- All terms and details of the agreement
- Conditions on which those terms are based

- Referenced material, such as price lists, warranty information, or insurance policies
- Important deadlines—both yours and the counterparty's
- Costs, prices, percentages, and other terms and conditions
- Remedies for nonperformance or altered performance
- Terms for terminating and/or renegotiating the contract

Get a Third Party? A Lawyer?

It often helps to call in a third party to write the contract—a business colleague, a contract specialist, or even a lawyer for a complex deal. The third party is impartial and can focus on the details of the deal. It is a best practice to have that person there through the negotiations to take their own notes and get a flavor for the deal.

Whether or not a lawyer writes the contract, a brief review from a lawyer is usually a good idea. The fees are probably minor and the expertise can be invaluable. Lawyers can spot mistakes, omissions, and uncertainties and can make the language more watertight where needed.

These tips, of course, don't apply to all situations. Use your own judgment and get agreement from the rest of your team and your counterparty as to whom to bring into an agreement.

ARE VERBAL CONTRACTS ENFORCEABLE?

It's a critical question in today's rapid business context. Many contracts can come about from a simple phone call or golf course conversation. State laws vary, but the baseline answer is "yes," verbal contracts are enforceable in most states. If there is an offer, consideration, and acceptance, the contract is generally enforceable, with certain exceptions such as real estate contracts.

Naturally, it helps to document the terms of the deal after the verbal agreement; otherwise enforcement can be difficult. If you do a lot of agreements on the fly, it's worth consulting an attorney to see whether your deals are in fact contracts. It's important to realize that a commitment you make by phone, text, or some other means also may be enforceable, even if you don't intend it to be.

GETTING THE DETAILS RIGHT

The agreement and ensuing contract should spell out all details of agreed-to actions and compensation, terms for termination or change, and in some cases, consequences for breach or violation of terms.

Contingencies

In addition, you should understand what happens if something unexpected occurs. If there's a fire and the production facility is damaged before the job is done, how will you proceed? Will the contract become null and void?

Consideration

Consideration is a fancy term for tangible compensation or promises. As a standard principle of contract law, a contract is only legal and valid if something of value is exchanged for something else of value and both parties agree on all the terms. Even further, some states require that consideration must be in writing in order for the contract to be considered legally binding.

Consideration includes any form of compensation—usually cash but it can be other tangible items. As a general principle, you must do *something* for the other party to be able to require the other party to do something for you or else it isn't really a contract.

What Does "Failure of Consideration" Mean?

Failure of consideration signifies the contract is breached; you or the other party didn't hold up your part of the bargain. For example, if you don't deliver a required deposit payment, the contract technically becomes null and void, and the person who has been wronged can withhold making good on *her* considerations and/or take legal action against the other party (you).

Contract Review

When the time comes to finalize the contract, careful review is important. It is a good idea to have an impartial colleague and/or attorney go over it for details, commitments, remedies, and possible omissions. If something needs to be changed, have both parties initial all changes and sign every page.

Review and rework the contract as many times as you need to until you're completely satisfied. However, don't overwork it—you don't want to renegotiate anything unless absolutely necessary.

When the final contract has been drawn up and all amendments have been settled, there should be one final meeting with you, the counterparty, and anyone else involved in drafting the final contract.

EXPECTING THE UNEXPECTED

Contract Remedies

Assuming the deal was negotiated in good faith, and assuming that both parties are up to completing their end of the deal and that there are no significant "mitigating circumstances" during the performance of the negotiated deal, all's well. If so, then what follows doesn't come into play. But negotiators and deal makers are all aware of—or should be aware of—what can happen if a negotiated contract goes awry. That knowledge, of course, helps negotiators work toward making a more foolproof deal in the first place.

Contract law holds parties accountable for neglecting to satisfy their part of the deal. Suppose you and a counterparty agree that in one week you will buy his car for $5,000. You explain that you'll need to sell your current car to get the $5,000. After the week is up and your car is sold, you go back to the car owner only to discover he's already sold the car to someone else for $6,000.

Though a written contract may not exist, a verbal promise was made in which you and the other party agreed to the details specified. You made plans based on that agreement; and contract law protects your right to perform acts contingent on those promises. It holds the other party responsible for failing to make good on a promise. Of course, if there's a written contract your chances of proving your case are far greater.

WITHDRAWING FROM THE CONTRACT

Most of us have experienced buyer's remorse. You find something you like, buy it, then change your mind. When you enter into a business contract, a lot depends on what the other party is willing to do. If you want to get out of the contract, the other party might allow it in order to maintain the integrity of the relationship. Maybe there was an oversight or something unexpected happened and your counterparty feels that cutting you loose is a better choice than enforcing the contract. Though your counterparty may empathize with your reasons for wanting to cancel the contract, they're not obliged to let you do it.

The Cooling-Off Rule

In its "cooling-off" rule, the Federal Trade Commission (FTC) states that if you purchase an item of $25 or more at a location away from the retailer's permanent address and you change your mind about the transaction, you're entitled to a full refund within three days of the date of purchase.

The rule applies to any sales that were made from a private home, a trade show, a hotel room, or restaurant. There are many exceptions to this rule, which can be reviewed at www.ftc.gov. This rule is a good example of the kinds of legal principles and precedents that might enter into your negotiating and deal making. And having a resource to discuss such matters is a good reason to take your attorney to lunch from time to time.

BREACH, AND HOW TO HANDLE IT

A breach happens when one party fails to perform what the contract states. For any breach you must decide its significance, whether it be a quality failure, delivery failure, or anything else. Of course, taking the matter to court for remedy will cost money and time.

For example, if your counterparty delivered goods three days past the agreed-upon ship date and the late shipment didn't harm your business, you wouldn't consider it a breach although you might discuss the matter with the counterparty. If, on the other hand, the breach is too significant to ignore, then there are many options available.

Specific Performance

In a court of law, the defendant may be ordered to deliver "specific performance"—that is, to complete the terms of the contract rather than, or in addition to, paying damages.

This form of ruling is fairly rare and is reserved mainly for real estate cases in which the seller changes his mind and doesn't want to go through with the promise made to the buyer. If "specific performance" is granted, the offending party will be ordered to deliver the goods, perform the job, or make the payment required in the contract.

Consequential and Incidental Damages

There are many creative ways to get what was promised, and most, not surprisingly, involve money. In addition to assessing the value of your losses, the judge might require the other party to pay attorney fees or "consequential and incidental damages"—money awarded for predictable losses related to a breach. Going back to the car sale example, since the car owner knew you were selling your old car to pay for the car he was selling you, and he sold the car to someone else, you might be entitled to some damage payments because he was aware of the contingency. How much damage payment is rewarded is typically up to the judge unless you can prove specific damages.

What Is a Tort?

A tort is similar to a breach of contract, but it usually concerns damages beyond the terms of the contract. This damage might relate to reputation of a party, or it might affect the physical ability of one of the parties to do something. It's a civil wrongdoing requiring a remedy from the court beyond the terms of the contract.

Rescission and Annulment

Other remedies pertain to the state of the contract itself. If the judge decides on a rescission of the contract, the contract is canceled, all advancements are to be paid back, and all parties are no longer responsible for their portion of the terms.

While you cannot be exonerated from poor business arrangements, judges will, in certain cases, annul an illegal contract. For example, if a sixteen-year-old signs a contract to buy a car, the contract is not binding because he is a minor and needs parental consent to sign it.

WHAT CAN VOID A CONTRACT?

Legal Escapes from Signed Contracts

Contract law generally holds that contracts can be invalidated under certain conditions where willful misrepresentation has occurred. Essentially, being fully up front and truthful is best, although a bit of salesperson's hyperbole or exaggeration on more subjective attributes ("These widgets are the best you can buy!") won't get you into too much trouble. But to "negotiate a lie" by willfully misrepresenting facts or attributes can be another matter.

GOOD FAITH OR BAD FAITH?

When two or more parties enter a negotiation, it is assumed that all parties involved will be honorable and live up to their contractual commitments. Good faith also implies that everyone will be fair and truthful to satisfy the purpose of the meeting. When a counterparty makes concessions they don't intend to live up to, they are acting in bad faith; a deal can be rendered null and void if bad faith is judged to be extensively present enough to influence the outcome of the negotiation.

Misrepresentation and Duress

If the other party tells you something he knows is false, and you sign the contract based on your belief that his statement is true, you can have the contract rescinded in court. The same holds true even if the other party was unaware that the information was false. Keep in mind that if you have the contract canceled, you'll be required to give back any consideration you received. This includes money, products, keys to the company car, and warranties, to name a few.

Similarly, if you signed a contract under duress (at gunpoint is the extreme example, or perhaps while seriously ill) the contract won't be considered a legal document. A contract can only be valid if both parties willingly agree to its terms. It cannot be enforced if one party is made to do something he would not have done under ordinary conditions.

Fraud

According to the *Merriam-Webster's Dictionary of Law*, the legal definition of *fraud* is "an intentional perversion of truth for the purpose of obtaining some valuable thing or promise from another." Similar to misrepresentation, fraud is an act in which a person presents false information, causing a counterparty to suffer a loss. The differences: fraud is intentional, and it is a criminal offense.

RESOLVING A DISPUTE

Sometimes a misunderstanding simply won't go away, and the specter of litigation enters the picture. Filing a lawsuit is a decision that shouldn't be made in haste, and legal advice is important at this point. The litigation process differs state by state and is beyond the scope of this book. Nonetheless, here are a few processes that can help you to bypass formal litigation as a solution to resolving agreement and contract disputes.

Alternative Dispute Resolutions

Before resorting to litigation, contract law provides for alternative methods for resolving disputes outside of court. Many of these methods involve some of the same negotiating skills that got you into the deal in the first place. Alternative dispute resolutions are, not surprisingly, geared toward resolving the dispute without the time, expense, and possible reputation damage of litigation. Three methods are available: negotiation and settlement, mediation, and arbitration.

Negotiation and Settlement

Negotiation and settlement is a return to the negotiation table for the two parties originally involved. The negotiation is reopened, the "sticking points" are resolved, and the counterparties come to a new agreement or an amendment to the existing one. No third party is formally involved, although one or both counterparties may choose to bring in someone neutral to moderate the discussion.

Mediation

Mediation involves the intervention of a third party, a mediator brought in to formally lead the discussion. While this can be someone highly knowledgeable in the issues being negotiated or mediated, that expertise often isn't necessary. However, the mediator should be professional, with expertise in the area of dispute resolution. The mediator's job is to actively help the disputing parties find a way to reach an agreement (not just to lead the meeting), especially when the negotiation is deadlocked.

The mediator offers a fresh perspective on the situation. That insight can help the disputing parties work toward a possible solution. Because the mediator works for both parties, she doesn't have a strong desire to hold on to certain concessions or make demands. Instead, the mediator tries to find the best possible win-win outcome based on the facts and objectives of the concerned parties.

Mediation is not a legal proceeding like a trial; the mediator cannot decide on what the parties must agree to. It's a casual meeting in which the mediator talks to both parties together and separately to refocus their attention on goals and ways to reach them.

Mediators are brought into negotiations and disputes to avoid litigation. If a lawsuit has already been filed, they might be brought in to avoid accruing more lawyer and court costs. Since all parties involved share the mediator's fees, mediation can often be the most favorable and cost-effective choice.

Like the contract resulting from a negotiation, the mediated agreement is documented, signed, and enforceable by law. If the agreement is reached after a lawsuit has been filed, the court will receive a copy and the case can be dismissed.

Arbitration

Arbitration is similar to mediation in that it is a type of alternative dispute resolution that involves the inclusion of an outside party to help settle the dispute. In this case, however, the arbitrator directs a hearing and then decides the outcome. It almost amounts to litigation but is faster, cheaper, and more flexible. You don't have to worry about the court calendar and docket, and the parties can decide on the rules in effect throughout the arbitration period.

For example, evidence that otherwise might not be allowed in court can be submitted in arbitration. Moreover, the parties can decide on who the arbitrators will be and whether the arbitration will be binding (parties must follow the arbitrator's final decisions) or nonbinding (parties take the final decisions under advice but do not have to carry them out). Once the arbitration is finished, the resulting decision cannot be appealed. The conflict is considered resolved, and the case is closed.

Who Can Be an Arbitrator?

Anyone can be an arbitrator so long as both parties agree. Typically, arbitrators are experts on the subject being discussed or are trusted community members (such as spiritual leaders) or are individuals who have many years of experience in law (such as retired judges or lawyers).

When choosing an arbitrator, look for a candidate with subject expertise who also possesses good written, oral, and organization skills. The individual should have the ability to summarize information quickly and make effective decisions. It helps to review the track record of the arbitrator. An ideal candidate will have experience congruent with your situation and a history of fast, friendly, and effective resolutions of similar disputes.

Chapter 11

Negotiating for the Long Term

Up to this point you've read about the strategies, tactics, pitfalls, and mechanics of a fast, friendly, and effective negotiation. You get that the best approach is a win-win, and that the biggest secret to success is preparation. You've adopted a negotiating style and you've learned to deal with the styles of others. You have the tools to approach any negotiation—whether it is with a business counterparty or your own teenager—with confidence and style.

However, over time, seasoned, career-minded negotiators, including the rest of us for whom negotiation isn't our main job but an adjunct to the job we do, realize that negotiating isn't just about working out the deal. It is about building and nourishing long-term relationships as well as a long-term reputation as a fair, effective negotiator.

Who you are as a negotiator can have a lot to do with who you become as a professional. Why? Two reasons. First and most obvious, if you can negotiate effectively you and your organization can get what you both need or want as deals are made going forward. Second, your reputation as an effective and fair dealmaker precedes you to the negotiating table, which enhances your standing as a professional and also builds trust and respect from your counterparties. This in turn makes every negotiation faster, friendlier, and more effective. It's a positive cycle, with you as beneficiary.

This concluding chapter suggests ways you can go beyond making the deal to cultivate a favorable negotiating reputation and competence for the long term.

REMEMBER, IT'S ALL ABOUT TRUST

Trust Is a Relationship Baseline

As in many aspects of life, both personal and professional, establishing and maintaining trust is a key baseline to doing anything else. Put differently, without trust, you might still win the negotiation, but it will be so much harder. Trust pushes a lot of the negative aside in a relationship, while no trust puts the negative front and center. For this reason, building and establishing trust should be one of your first and foremost goals, both at work and outside of it.

The best way to bring trust to a negotiation is to have it as part of your reputation coming in. For new negotiators, that can be more difficult. You build trust through friendly rapport, through reinforcing the idea of win-win, and by showing you're not just "in it to win it" so that you can move on as quickly as possible. You're honest, forthcoming, communicative, and you work collaboratively to develop solutions that work. You keep your word, make promises that are kept, and are easy to work with.

Your words and actions demonstrate your reliability and commitment. You walk the walk rather than just talk the talk. Just saying, "You can trust me" doesn't sound very convincing. Worse, some may assume the opposite upon hearing this. You realize that your sincerity will be compromised if you come off too strong or too eager to make a good impression. You avoid passive-aggressive behavior. You are yourself, not a made-up character or persona. You do what's necessary to avoid making the counterparty skeptical.

Set the Dial to Win-Win

I've mentioned this repeatedly but it bears restating. In any negotiation you want the counterparty to feel comfortable working with you right from the beginning. The first and most obvious way is to reinforce the win-win paradigm. Explain that both of you have much more to gain by working together instead of against each other. If the other party agrees, great. If you get resistance or if he just seems skeptical, assure him that a win-win solution is the fastest, easiest, and best way to accomplish your goals—it's been proven millions of times through human history.

SPEAK SOFTLY, SPEAK FIRST, AND BE APPROACHABLE

The atmosphere you create, especially in the beginning of a negotiation, can influence your counterparty's decision about whether to trust you. If you break the ice by speaking first, you'll have the advantage of setting a positive tone. You can show a calm, friendly, inviting demeanor. Speak softly, invite questions, and direct the conversation with confidence.

It's about Time

In today's fast-paced business world, time is of the essence, not only for the negotiation itself but also for the negotiating parties. It's good to acknowledge that up front, and set not only the ground rules but a general tone that fast is good. In effect, you are making a mutual pact not to waste each other's time.

And of course, with trust and a win-win mentality, "fast" is more likely to happen; you can do more in a shorter period of time.

No matter how much knowledge or leverage you have, throwing your weight around will only succeed in distancing your counterparty. Instead, be approachable. Express your feelings about any issue or possible outcome you don't agree with, but be sure to stay in control of your emotions, remaining calm and collected. Talk about why something doesn't work for you, and look for a solution that does. Portraying a positive attitude shows the other party that you're willing to look at problems from every angle in order to get to the bottom of them.

The more you open up, the more you show your honest side and the more they'll trust you. If you want the counterparty to let his guard down a little, you'll have to do the same.

Keep Your Sense of Humor

Laughter is a great way to lighten up the mood in any situation, and it also gets people talking again. If you're stuck on an issue and you both feel you've exhausted every possible angle, find a way to joke about it. You'll begin to loosen up and hopefully be able to move on with the topic you're discussing.

But don't be too silly, off color, or persistent with it. Other parties will question your seriousness or worse, take offense.

SAY WHAT YOU'LL DO, DO WHAT YOU SAY

Outside of the golden rule (treat others as you wish to be treated yourself), I can't think of nine other more prescient and important words to describe a successful modus operandi in life. Say what you're going to do and do what you say consistently, and how could people *not* trust you?

When people say they'll get back to you, isn't it nice when they actually do? There is no better feeling than when you can depend on someone consistently, whether in a business or personal relationship. In contrast, when people don't do what they say they're going to do—or don't state clearly what they're going to do in the first place (another passive-aggressive behavior observed all too frequently) you lose trust quickly.

Further, "Do what you say" must be always on. If you come through nine times and fail the tenth, you'll blow it on trust even though you might consider yourself 90 percent trustworthy.

Reputation Is a Fragile Thing

Building trust is about saying what you'll do and doing what you'll say. It's also about doing what you say consistently. Billionaire investor Warren Buffett said it best: "It takes you twenty years to build a reputation and five minutes to destroy it."

Never forget that trust is an always-on proposition.

IT'S A COLLABORATIVE EFFORT

Once you and the other party have established trust, you'll have an easier time working together without worrying about being manipulated by each other. With each subsequent negotiation, this trust will grow deeper, and you'll be able to open up to each other even more. It all leads to faster, friendlier, and more effective negotiated solutions.

Beyond that, good negotiators know that the combined knowledge of all parties involved is more useful than that of only one party. Good negotiators are inclusive of everyone in the room, and aren't afraid to bring in experts. Everybody has a chance to share their expertise and voice their opinions; nothing is left unsaid or held from view. At the end of the day, this is just another way to build trust.

Don't Make Empty Promises

Always avoid making promises you aren't sure you can keep. If someone asks you a question that you can't answer, say that you'll look into the issue—and *do* it. Each time you make good on a promise, whether big or small, it will be remembered. Live up to your end of the deal consistently and you'll enhance your reputation. Let things fall through the cracks and you'll ruin it.

Never forget that people remember!

Conflict Resolution

A key indicator of success for you as a negotiator and for the negotiating teams in general is how you and they handle conflicts. It starts, of course, with a good interpersonal relationship between counterparties—when the going gets tough, open lines of communication can save the day.

Resolving conflicts starts with clearly identifying them. Countless times negotiating teams have wasted time solving the wrong problem, for instance, haggling over price when the real issue was quality. Conflict resolution should start with a clear identification of the problem, followed by agreed-to steps to resolve it (sort of a mini-agenda within the agenda). Clear communication and an adherence to win-win principles is vital. Perhaps most important is not to take the conflict personally and, as always, to separate the people from the problem. Trying to blame a member of one of the teams for a conflict will get you nowhere.

POWER OF EXAMPLE, NOT EXAMPLES OF POWER

This paraphrased Bill Clinton quote says a lot about maintaining a collaborative, win-win stance while still getting what you need out of a negotiation. Loosely defined, power is the ability to influence others and to get their recognition. When I say "influencing others," I mean it in the leadership sense—getting others to think something or want to do something—not in the control sense. Win-win is leadership, win-lose is intimidation and control.

There's a difference between "good power" and "bad power." Power through reputation and accomplishment is much more effective than power through coercion. Good power is more real and long lasting than power gained by intimidation, harsh language, "loud" body language, or even position title. Both types of power can get results, but the one that wins long term is achievement-based power. As I boil it down in my book *What Would Steve Jobs Do?*, achievement can lead to power, but power rarely leads to achievement.

Where is all of this going? Shouting and carrying on—examples or demonstrations of power—might work in the short term to manipulate individuals in the negotiation. But their effects are short-lived and ultimately breed resentment, often shifting the balance of power in the other direction. Power by example—setting a positive tone, letting your achievements and reputation speak for themselves—has a far longer-lasting effect.

Power can be the "secret sauce" of a negotiation, making it all go well and providing a favorable outcome that nurtures a positive long-term relationship. Power can also poison the well permanently if abused. Use power with caution, and if you have it, don't flaunt it.

CREATING LASTING RELATIONSHIPS

Playing for the Long Term

Although many negotiations will seem to be short-term one-offs, you never know what business opportunity might come up next. You may even have to renegotiate parts of a deal if something changes along the way. As a consequence, even if it doesn't seem like creating a lasting relationship is relevant, it still pays to do so. You never know whether you'll work with the same counterparties again; furthermore, your reputation can spread like wildfire—if you're a jerk during this negotiation because you're sure you'll never see these folks again, that reputation can easily spread to someone you *will* see again. It's a small world, and news travels fast.

That being the case, it's always a good idea to treat a negotiating or business relationship, even one generated in a simple phone call or email dialogue, as if it's a long-term relationship. You just never know.

REACHING A COMFORT ZONE

Once you've been working with someone for a while, you reach a point at which you both feel comfortable enough to make suggestions without worrying about how the other will react to them. You've reached a comfort zone; trust has taken over, and the negotiation can proceed on its own objective merits without the natural skepticism between new or untested participants.

This is important, for it allows you to say what really needs to be said without fear of something being taken personally and damaging the relationship or the negotiation. Every step of every negotiation, in fact, is really just another event in a long-term relationship. As such, the parties understand and trust each other, and no single conflict or difference or misspoken word can destroy it.

It Doesn't Hurt to Stay in Touch

Once the negotiation is complete, do you simply walk away and wait for the next contract or deal renewal? You shouldn't.

In the interest of the long-term relationship, you should touch base occasionally to make sure everything is proceeding with your deal as it should. Make contact often enough to ensure expected performance and to enhance goodwill, but not so often as to be annoying. Good big-ticket retail salespeople have figured this out. A phone call, email, or text every few months or so can do a lot to preserve and build the relationship—and to make things easier the next time around.

SHARPENING YOUR NEGOTIATING "SAW"

Every negotiation is a learning experience. You should always come out of a negotiation feeling as if you've gained a little more: more effective techniques; strategies and tactics; and a stronger reputation and relationship with your counterparties, and, for that matter, the rest of your team and management chain. You learn how to present your side, resolve conflicts, and to put together working documents and contracts from your negotiations. Practice makes perfect, and the only way to become a "perfect" negotiator is to, well, *negotiate*.

After a while you'll clearly recognize what worked and what didn't work in any given negotiation. It isn't a bad idea to list what did and didn't work in each negotiation, and perhaps note the three best and three worst things you did or didn't do. Keep track of these summaries in a safe place where you can review them from time to time. If you see the same three worst items over and over, you know the areas where you have work to do.

You Might Think It Was a Mistake. They Didn't.

Public speakers know that while they may beat themselves up for something they forgot to say, the audience doesn't know what they didn't say. If you forget to bring up a point in a negotiation, but it doesn't materially affect the outcome, nobody else will ever know. If it did affect the outcome, well, lesson learned; perhaps you could have been better prepared or organized for the day of the show.

Look at yourself for what others saw. And remember, it's about results, not your performance per se.

You might consider using a grading system to measure your success. Don't beat yourself up over what you could've and should've done, but do critique your performance fairly and objectively. How well did you prepare? How effective was your style? How quickly were you able to adapt to changes? Would you consider your relationship with the counterparty a good one?

Don't be too harsh on yourself. You want to learn from it, not punish yourself. Recognize that no matter how badly you felt you did, there most likely were some *good things* you did as well. We naturally tend to dwell on the negative, and we tend to become defensive in an effort to protect who we are and what we do from criticism. For each negotiation, take inventory; separate the good from the bad. Celebrate the good and learn from the bad. The glass half empty is also half full.

THE "A" LIST

Perhaps it is obvious by now, but every negotiation you'll be engaged in involves roughly the same set of key skills and steps. You can set up a simple grading chart covering just a handful of items. What follows is an example of a short chart you might use to grade or score your performance in a negotiation:

- You "saw" the negotiation: its preparation, start, middle, and finish.
- You prepared the right—and right amount of—information, including product attributes, competitive environment, etc.
- You "knew" the counterparty and what she or he was looking for.
- You got the deal done.
- You achieved your objectives and goals.
- You came up with a win-win.
- You have a good idea of what went right and what went wrong.
- You learned from your mistakes.
- You advanced the relationship with these negotiators.
- You advanced your personal and professional reputation.

You won't get straight A's the first time around; nobody does. But over time your grades will inevitably improve.

ENJOYING THE RIDE

You'll be surprised at how much enjoyment you derive from a negotiation well done. Not only do you get the opportunity to achieve goals and do something important, you get to work with (and learn from) some talented and skilled people. Together, you and your counterparty will embark on a journey of discovery and creativity in finding a win-win solution and developing an effective plan around it. You've enhanced your reputation and a relationship; and the bonds you formed will help lead to agreements and further the possibility of future commitments.

And you've inevitably learned from the experience.

INDEX

A

evasive/uncooperative, 102–3
expressive/communicative,
104–5
friendly/collaborative, 99–102
logical/analytical, 97–99
negotiation styles and, 72. *See
also* Styles, negotiating
passive-aggressiveness and,
96–97, 101, 103, 106, 152, 180,
234
passive/submissive, 95–97
playing defense with, 95, 97, 99,
102, 103, 105
Pitfalls, to avoid, 155–75
about: overview of, 155
allowing stress to take over,
163–65; 174–75
avoiding negotiating, 171
case study illustrating, 173–75
failing to "see" win-win, 156–57
forgetting human element,
158–62
mishandling concessions,
166–68
not bringing up grey areas/mis-
takes, 169–70
not keeping objectives in focus,
171–72
personal agendas, 159–60
wrong risks, 170–71
Ploys. *See* Stagecraft for negotiating; Tactics references
Positional negotiating, 37–39, 84,
95, 197
Positivity
encouragement, enthusiasm
and, 205–6
flatterers and, 78

keeping sense of humor and,
233
leadership and, 207–8
overcoming negativity, 199
personal agendas, being the
"white hat" and, 159
power of example and, 236–37
productive communication and,
198, 199
setting atmosphere for negotiation, 232–33
stress, breaks and, 174–75
word selection and, 161
Power of example vs. examples of
power, 236–37
Preparation and planning, 45–71.
See also Goals; Visualizing
about: overview of, 45
additional time for, 125–26
agenda for meeting, 65–66
alternatives (BATNA). *See* Alternatives
case study illustrating, 68–71
fast prep vs. full prep, 64
for/using concessions, 54–56.
See also Concessions
knowing counterparties, 57–60
knowing must and wants, 50–51
knowing your limitations and
weaknesses, 52–53
for meeting itself, 65–67
Pareto Principle (80-20 rule)
and, 64
readying for the game, 46
"scouts motto," 164
starting with the end in mind,
47–48, 51, 207–9
value and importance of, 45

when you're not ready, 125–26
Professional negotiators, 29
Promises, empty, 235

Q

R

S

V

W

ABOUT THE AUTHOR

Peter Sander (Granite Bay, California) is an author, researcher, and consultant in the fields of personal finance, business leadership, innovation management, and location reference. He has written forty-eight books, including the annual 100 Best Stocks to Buy series, *What Would Steve Jobs Do?*, *All about Low Volatility Investing*, *Value Investing for Dummies*, *The 25 Habits of Highly Successful Investors*, *101 Things Everyone Should Know about Economics*, and *Cities Ranked & Rated*. He is also the author of numerous articles and columns on investment strategies. He has an MBA from Indiana University and has completed Certified Financial Planner (CFP) education and examination requirements.